The original pl
with updates to
Clayton. This 2013 court ruling initiated
transfers across Missouri based on district accreditation status. In preparation for the re-release, I was able to locate some powerful, never told stories from those intimately involved and witnessed the impact of student transfers on themselves and on public education. The book cover was finalized, a promotion strategy was created, and a tentative release date was selected. But then something happened that many of us familiar with the intersection of public education, politics, and its impact on Black school communities know all too well. History began to repeat itself.

In March 2023, Missouri House Bill 253 (Student Transfer) passed and moved to the Missouri Senate. This bill, known as Open Enrollment, establishes transfer procedures to nonresident districts for students in public schools.

Though this was not the first or second attempt at state-wide Open Enrollment, one could only think that sooner or later, such persistence would result in one of these open enrollment bills being passed.

Intrigued, I deeply investigated the bill, the hearings, support, opposition, and increasing media coverage. What was discovered felt like the continuation of my dissertation completed six years ago. Furthermore, publishing a book on student transfers without including this rapidly evolving matter felt like a powerful story being truncated at a critical time. There was so much more to share about the same Black communities still recovering from the impact of student transfers. The latest iteration of student transfers, which included language that would toe the line of legalized discriminatory practices in accepting and denying students, was like watching the newest tactic to further denigrate school communities in which Black students reside.

Since integration following the 1954 Brown vs. Board of Education decision, semantics and fine print found in laws and policies along with good intentions from organizations, politicians, and school leaders have consistently rendered an outcome so predictable that we know precisely how the book ends.

TRANSFERS & OPEN ENROLLMENT
The Denigration of Black School Communities

Copyright © 2023 Dr. Howard E. Fields III LLC
All rights reserved.

This book is available at significant quantity discounts when purchased in bulk for educational use. For inquiries and details, contact me@drhowardfields.com or 314.643.6393.

Cover and design by Howard E. Fields III, Ph.D.
Editing by MMG Edits

The web addresses and QR codes referenced in this book were live and correct at publication but may be subject to change.

Library of Congress Control Number: 2023910075
Paperback ISBN: 978-1-7369318-5-1
eBook ISBN: 978-1-7369318-6-8

Transfers & Open Enrollment
The Denigration of Black School Communities

TABLE OF CONTENTS

- Acknowledgements   vi
- Preface   vii
- Foreword   ix
  Dr. Chris Lee Nicastro - Former Missouri Commissioner of Education

PART I

- Setting the Stage for Student Transfers   1
  Elise Tomich - Former St. Louis Post-Dispatch Education Reporter
- Introduction   6
- How It Started   9
- Case Study   37
- Processing the Case Study   72

PART II

- From A Communications Perspective   99
  I. Melanie Powell Robinson - Former Riverview Gardens School District Executive Director of Communications
  II. Neosha Bowles - Former Francis Howell School District Communication Technology Specialist
- Race & School Rankings   119
- The Cost of The Student Transfer Program   126
- New Missouri Accountability Measure   128
- Open Enrollment   137
- The Denigration of Black School Communities   145

v

Acknowledgments

To Drs. Carl Hoagland, Keith Miller, Lynn Beckwith Jr., and the late Matthew Davis, when I started this research ten years ago, you told me that history must be written honestly, boldly, and unapologetically. With respect to this topic, I believe I did just that. Thank you for pushing me to share a story worth sharing with the world. Both now and for years to come.

To my wife and children, thank you for your sacrifice. I love you more than anything in this world.

Preface

Sometimes I wonder what type of educator I would have been if my journey was different. Suppose I had never taught or led in under-resourced schools with overly enforced standardized testing measures, a space where you gave better than your best effort every day if you wanted your students to have a chance at being successful. For the first nine years of my educational career, this was home. I loved being part of teams that had no choice but to chase the most ambitious goals. We didn't see students as academic achievement levels based on their state assessment results. We saw students that possessed apparent, as well as hidden, gifts. Their potential was immeasurable. If I never had these experiences, I would quite possibly view education differently. Maybe I would not have such passion and urgency for this work. Perhaps I would smile and hang out more with colleagues who have never been in such a predicament. Maybe I would have less frustration knowing the rules typically do not benefit the students attempting to navigate the same schools I attended as a younger person. I often envision a profession where you are not viewed as abrasive for expecting that all students be treated as intellectuals. A profession where individuals who have zero experience increasing quantitative measures for Black students are not considered experts or provided so much power and autonomy to determine what students need. Given how schools are typically run, such framing may require quite a bit of unlearning. Whenever I speak with current or aspiring teachers and leaders, I convey that our students do not need fixing. Nor do they need more overly empathic yet underly actionable educators tasked with ensuring their success. They need more of us to challenge existing systems detrimental to their success. They need more school systems to remove barriers that preclude them from adequate access. They need educational policies that do not punish them for living in a particular part of town while incentivizing living in more affluent communities. The type of policies that refrain from robbing them of opportunities and resources. As someone who pays close attention to public educational policies, particularly those that impact Black schools and communities, I have grown increasingly critical of policies. Over time, the impact of many educational policies forced me to question if there was a more sinister intent. Either we are terrible at writing laws that uplift Black students and communities, or we are masterful at writing regulations that will cause further harm to Black students and communities. I initially wrote Part I of this book as my dissertation to focus on the immediate impact of an educational policy, the Student Transfer Law. The additions to my research focus on the long-term implications of this law from existing and new perspectives. Add a dose of open enrollment, combined with more educational policy, and the result is a book that takes a closer look into Missouri's student transfers and open enrollment attempts. I hope such an examination will help others understand my journey as an educator while also forcing us to consider the lasting impact of our collective action, as well as inaction for the sake of our students and community.

Howard E. Fields III, Ph.D.

Foreword

> *"There is no such thing as a neutral education process. Education either functions as an instrument which is used to facilitate the integration of generations into the logic of the present system and bring about conformity to it, or it becomes the 'practice of freedom', the means by which men and women deal critically with reality and discover how to participate in the transformation of their world."*
>
> *- Paulo Freire*

When Howard asked me to write this foreword, I had mixed feelings. I was flattered, of course, and gratified that he thought my perspective might add to his extensively researched book. I was also terrified...and angry...and profoundly sad. Why are we still writing about this? Why do we keep spending money, wasting time, and—most damning of all—doing nothing significant to eradicate the systemic racism, the underfunding, and the educational malpractice that afflicts our community, especially our black children?

As a "North (St. Louis) County" educator, I spent 26 years working in districts with large minority populations. I witnessed firsthand the effects of white flight, neighborhood decay, and increasing levels of poverty and crime. I served children every day, some of whom were hungry, or who needed health care, or were homeless, or were victims of abuse in their own homes. I developed a strong passion for making a positive difference for our kids. All our kids. I also became increasingly enraged at the injustice and inequities I witnessed every day. I felt guilty that my own children, safely housed in a white community and a predominantly white school, were so privileged. I learned about racism and internalized oppression. And at the end of my formal career, I felt the burden of bad legislation, inadequate solutions, and insurmountable problems. Over decades, the region and the state had allowed inequity to flourish and established a system of regulations, laws, and organizations designed to maintain the status quo.

As you read this book, I want to call your attention specifically to an idea that emerged in 1981 and is referenced at the end of this book. In 1981, a federal judge called for a plan to bus black St. Louis children to white suburban schools. White suburban residents, and their school leaders, revolted. They laid down in front of buses, filed motions in court, and sent angry letters to the newspaper. The judge, William Hungate, responded by threatening to do the one thing the white suburbs feared more than the bussing plan: Dissolve the carefully constructed school district boundaries and merge all 24 of the discrete districts into a single metro-wide one. He even contemplated expanding the case to include Jefferson and St. Charles counties.

Stunned white suburban parents and politicians called for constitutional protection. On July 5, 1983, Hungate approved a massive voluntary student-transfer program across the city-county line and ordered the state of Missouri to pay for it. The suburban districts signed on, seeking to avoid what they considered a worse fate.

The impact of this has been mixed, a point clearly made herein by the interviews with parents and students who participated in the transfer program. Many black students found great opportunity and success in their predominantly white suburban schools. Many white students benefitted from having black students in their classes. But many were left behind. And students left behind were further disadvantaged by the financial drain on the St. Louis Public Schools. Already financially secure County districts reaped the benefits of this fiscal bonanza.

As populations moved West and North, several North County school districts already had black populations over 25%, making them ineligible to participate in the voluntary program. Others dropped out as their black populations grew past 25%. While these districts' black populations increased, they—unlike other County districts—received no additional money from the state to address their needs. North County districts, and St. Louis City, faced significant financial challenges in meeting the needs of a growing black population.

The second significant transfer program came about some years later, this time affecting children from Normandy and Riverview Gardens, and mandated by a state law which, by his own admission, the author said: "was never intended to be applied." His assumption was that underperforming districts could be improved by threat and by financial penalties. The disruption created by this program was significant. Jobs were lost, and students who didn't transfer were further disadvantaged by the loss of resources and programs.

As with the voluntary transfer program, the reactions were mixed. One leader in Normandy accused me of "blatantly and deliberately trying to destroy the community." One mother grabbed my hand and said,

"Thank you. I'm so grateful I don't have to send my babies to a bad school anymore." The only outcome anyone can attest to with certainty is that all our efforts have helped some students and hurt others. We have yet to figure out how to provide high-quality education for every child in an integrated system.

And now, as the transfer programs wind down and districts—significantly improved or not—have regained their accreditation, the region again reflects the segregated status that the Supreme Court ruled unconstitutional 70 years ago. Our black and white student populations are increasingly separate, and their educational experience and opportunity is not equal.

In reflecting on these 40 years after the first voluntary transfer program began, I can't help but speculate what would have happened if, in fact, the suburban districts had been consolidated into one. Imagine a district with area schools, each area with diverse populations, sufficient funds to serve all children, and governing structures committed to true "excellence and equity." Such a district might have a chance of making this tired and meaningless phrase actually come to life.

Perhaps someday, there will be the willingness, the courage, and the political will to make this kind of systemic, radical change a reality.

Chris Lee Nicastro, Ph.D.

Former Missouri Commissioner of Education, Former Hazelwood School District Superintendent, and Former Riverview Gardens School District Superintendent

PART I

Setting the Stage for Student Transfers

The call came during lunch with friends in June of 2013. It was my editor. You should get back to the newsroom, he said. The Missouri Supreme Court had just upheld the school transfer law.

I was one of two education reporters at the St. Louis Post-Dispatch and pulled up the ruling on my phone. The implications were clear. Thousands of children in the state's lowest performing school districts would have the opportunity to receive a high-quality education. Superintendents throughout the region would have about 13 weeks to figure out how to enroll them. The two affected school districts – the Normandy and Riverview Gardens school systems in north St. Louis County – would be responsible for tuition and transportation costs.

A question lingered: would it change it anything?

For students in the Normandy and Riverview Gardens school districts, the ruling was a defining one. And one that would expose the racial, socio-economic and geographical divides that persist in the St. Louis area.

An exodus of 2,200 students – about a quarter of the enrollment – would leave the two districts that year. Most were African-American. Tens of millions of dollars from Normandy and Riverview Gardens would follow them into predominantly white and more affluent districts, draining both school systems of resources. Within months, Normandy faced insolvency. An elementary school would close. Class sizes ballooned. Gifted services and honors courses disappeared. Teachers lost their jobs. The communities within those districts faced the possibility that their schools might close for good.

The Missouri Supreme Court ruling presented a story that was high stakes and endlessly nuanced. A law with the best of intentions provided opportunity and also inflicted systemic harm at a level difficult to describe.

Students who transferred found classrooms with updated technology and materials, higher paid teachers, and more rigorous instruction. Students who didn't transfer remained in environments with no system or routines - and in districts also hemorrhaging millions of dollars.

One morning I walked to the bus stop with a transfer student from Riverview Gardens. She left home at 5:45 a.m. each morning carrying a 35-pound backpack from her shoulders. Regardless of weather, this high school senior walked more than a mile to the bus stop in the dark, for two years on streets without sidewalks, so she could get a ride to her new high school 30 miles away.

A former classmate of hers, an honors student at Normandy High School, began speaking out at public hearings about how budget cuts were affecting him. He planned to enroll in college, but the honors classes he needed to prepare him had been eliminated. Many of his teachers were so demoralized some had stopped bothering with lesson plans. By May of that year, he had not been assigned one single book to read.

For almost a generation, parents in the Normandy and Riverview Gardens school districts had hoped for better education options. The vast majority of students lived below the federal poverty line, creating desperation and strain in classrooms. Both districts had symptoms of the lingering effects of housing segregation and disinvestment that resulted as white families left north St. Louis County in the 1990s. In the 2000s, north St. Louis County was disproportionately hit by the subprime lending crisis. Plummeting home values hit school budgets hard and left many families underwater on their mortgages - making it impossible for anyone wanting different schools to move. By 2013, reading and math scores in Normandy and Riverview Gardens were the lowest in the state. They had been for years.

This was despite the best efforts of many talented educators. Throughout the years of student transfers, I met teachers and principals who poured everything they had into helping children overcome a system that wasn't designed for their success. One of these educators was Howard Fields, a new principal at Koch Elementary School in Ferguson. His first day of school at Koch came a few days after a police officer murdered Michael Brown, a Normandy High School grad, around the corner from the elementary school.

Those years made a profound impact on Dr. Fields, who has also worked at a Riverview Gardens middle school and later became an administrator in districts where transfer students attended. He built relationships with families whose stories represented the full spectrum of experiences during those years. Meanwhile, the racism that created education disparities in St. Louis persisted.

Shortly after the ruling, the Normandy superintendent chose one school district to send buses to – the destination for many white families that had left north St. Louis County as Black families moved in. Normandy transfer students who needed bus transportation would cross the Missouri River into St. Charles County and attend Francis Howell schools.

At a packed town hall meeting that summer, a drum beat of white parents went to a microphone and urged the Francis Howell superintendent to ignore the ruling and reduce class size targets for the sole purpose of stopping the incoming flow of transfer students. It was an explicit demonstration of racism. The Missouri NAACP threatened legal action if Francis Howell or any other school district appeared to be circumventing the law. Fortunately, superintendents across the region complied with the law and showed support for transfer students and their families.

Meanwhile, the author of the school transfer law said he never intended for it to go into effect. Harold Caskey, who served as a Democratic state senator from 1977 to 2004, said he wrote the law to provide the kind of accountability that would force Missouri's struggling school districts to improve and avoid academic failure. The law's financial consequences were intended to be so severe that failure wouldn't be an option, he told me repeatedly during an interview.

But a number of districts had failed anyway, including two of the largest school districts in the state – St. Louis Public Schools and Kansas City Public Schools. It was the lawsuit intended to force St. Louis districts to cover the cost of student transfers that ultimately went to the

Missouri Supreme Court. By the time the high court upheld the law, the state had upgraded the accreditation status of the St. Louis Public School District.

To be sure, the legacy of the school transfer law is complicated.

It created disruption. It changed circumstances for thousands of children, for better and for worse. Some Normandy and Riverview Gardens transfer students have graduated college - possibly because of the access to opportunity they received in higher performing schools. I remember sitting at kitchen tables and in living rooms listening to the dreams of parents determined to do all that they could to keep their children in their new schools.

Today, both districts continue to demonstrate the lowest math and reading scores in the state. The Missouri State Board of Education upgraded the accreditation status of Riverview Gardens in 2016, and Normandy in 2017. Children living in either district are no longer allowed to transfer to other schools.

Elise Tomich
Elise Tomich - Former St. Louis Post-Dispatch Education Reporter

Introduction

For over 70 years, Black students have been a case study for public educational policy initiatives. An insidious entanglement of racism, inequity, lack of funding, and disappointment requires a critical and longitudinal assessment for these otherwise hidden truths to emerge. Brown vs. Topeka Board of Education (1954) is considered foundational to educational equity due to the focus on racial integration within schools. It is seldom mentioned that the aftermath of this ruling resulted in thousands of Black teachers losing their jobs because Black schools were closed. Most references to Brown vs. Board also fail to mention that tens of thousands of Black students lost the ultimate sense of belonging when placed in predominantly White schools.

Liddell vs. St. Louis Public School Board of Education (1983) was initially viewed as a compromise to desegregate schools in St. Louis City and County. However, schools in St. Louis are more segregated today than forty years ago. Even the most well-intentioned, bipartisan, and adequately funded laws involving public education are too reactionary; the recipe of haphazardly addressing immediate issues without much regard for the long-term impact has been a consistent course of action for policymakers. In 1993, the state of Missouri passed the Outstanding Schools Act to ensure that "all children" receive quality educational opportunities regardless of where in Missouri they live. The accountability criterion of the Outstanding Schools Act birthed what would become known as the Student Transfer Law. A law that allowed students in an unaccredited school district to transfer to an accredited school district.

In 2013, the Breitenfeld vs. School District of Clayton decision would catapult The Student Transfer Law into action, making it the most significant education story in the region. Though bussing students from Black communities to White communities was not entirely new, requiring these already less-resourced school districts to pay transportation and tuition costs for student transfers was a more unknown, more challenging element.

June 11, 2023, marks ten years since the Breitenfeld vs. Clayton ruling. A decade presents an adequate opportunity to examine the long-term impact this educational policy has had on public education within the region, particularly in certain schools and communities. The long-term implications I speak of require an analysis from a patient yet knowledgeable individual with experience examining public educational policies. Specifically, policies that disproportionately impact Black schools and communities. Implementing the Student Transfer Law correlates with the beginning of my administrative career. In the summer of 2013, I spent countless hours calling the parents and guardians of my middle school students who I had worked closely with for two consecutive years. Call after the call, I sincerely pleaded with them to reconsider transferring from our unaccredited school district. Some stayed, but many did not. Later that year, I visited former students at their new school as part of an instructional walkthrough. You could not imagine the heartbreak I felt seeing some of them in the same resource classroom, knowing their academic potential should have placed them in a gifted or accelerated classroom. Moments like these for a new administrator serving in the same school community he once called home force you to see education differently. I did not have to turn on the news or read the St. Louis Post Dispatch to understand what was going on with the student transfer program. My colleagues, students, and community were all trying to navigate and make sense of this new public educational policy said to create a more equitable and quality educational experience for students from previously excluded groups.

The contrasting experiences I have obtained more recently as an administrator in predominantly White districts, along with a more robust understanding of racism, inequity, policy, and the lack of funding within the education field, have created a desire to pick up where my 2017 dissertation was left and provide an updated examination of The Student Transfer Law. In the following pages, you will shift back and forth between reader and researcher. As you process these powerful true stories, I ask that you critically examine not just this public educational policy but other ones within the context of its impact on Black schools and communities. By doing so, you may better understand the persistent exhaustion and disappointment from being yet another public education case study.

How It Started

During the summer of 2013, the Riverview Gardens School District, located in North St. Louis County, Missouri, was dealt a catastrophic blow that would leave the then-unaccredited school district on the brink of lapsing. According to Missouri State Statute 162.081, an unaccredited school district could lapse, which means that at any time, the Missouri School Board has the authority to dissolve the district and annex students to other school districts. So, when the Missouri Supreme Court ruled that unaccredited school districts had to pay for students who were interested in transferring to an accredited school district (Breitenfeld v. School District of Clayton, 2013), the challenge of regaining accreditation became much more difficult for the Riverview Gardens School District.

As a new Riverview Gardens administrator in 2013, I observed how the Breitenfeld v. School District of Clayton ruling impacted an entire district from the inside. Although many media reports focused on the financial, political, and school implications of student transfers, particular perspectives did not gain much attention, one being the different ways families reacted to the ruling. I was conversing with families about transferring during the summer of 2013. The June 11, 2013, ruling meant that families could transfer for the upcoming 2013-2014 school year, which was scheduled to start on August 12, 2013. Many Riverview Gardens administrators had strong relationships with district students and their families. To capitalize on these relationships, we began calling families who filed for transfer, passionately pleading for them to give the district and the incoming superintendent another year to reconsider transferring. For many families, being recruited to stay was enough to grant the district another opportunity; others respectfully declined our passionate pleas and decided to transfer. Ultimately, I just wanted what was best for my students and their families. At the time, given all the nuances, there was no way of knowing what the best option for them would be.

When I started formally researching the impact of the latest iteration of student transfers, it had been nearly five years since students began transferring from Riverview Gardens under what has become known as the Student Transfer Program. The first portion of this book consists of a case study. Parents of former Riverview Gardens students share their personal experiences and stories and the impact the Student Transfer Program had on their families.

Background

In educational policy, words such as "quality education," "improvement," or "maximizing opportunities" are used with great regularity. Take, for example, the Elementary and Secondary Education Act (ESEA). Signed into law by President Lyndon B. Johnson in 1965, the purpose of ESEA was to "strengthen and improve educational quality and educational opportunities in the Nation's elementary and secondary schools" (Elementary and Secondary Education Act of 1965). The State of Missouri echoed this mission in 1993 with the passing of the

Outstanding Schools Act. The mission of this act was to ensure that "all children have quality educational opportunities regardless of where in Missouri they live" (Outstanding Schools Act of 1993).

Notwithstanding the year, the narrative remains the same. A law that mandates equitable education is passed, only to have the interpretation and implementation decided in court. Liddell v. Board of Education in 1983 is a perfect example. Ironically, the twenty-eight years between ESEA and the Outstanding Schools Act represent the same number of years that Mrs. Minnie Liddell fought for equitable educational opportunities in the St. Louis Public School District (SLPSD).

Admitted as a slave state to the Union through the Missouri Compromise (1820), Missouri was the most northern state to require separate schools for Whites and Blacks (Gotham, 2002). Although Brown v. Board of Education (1954) abolished separate but equal practices, during the 1970s, "Black [SLPSD] students, [still] attended schools in old, dilapidated buildings, their textbooks were both used and outdated, [and] their classrooms were substantially overcrowded" (Norwood, 2012, p. 7). According to Dr. Lynn Beckwith Jr., former SLPSD student, former Superintendent of Schools in University City, and former President of the Special Administrative Board in the Riverview Gardens School District, these claims, however, could be disputed when considering the number of newly built schools that Black students attended in SLPSD during this time (L. Beckwith, personal communication, December 8, 2016). What cannot be disputed is how

Black students were often transported and reassigned from their neighborhood schools to other predominately Black schools across town, while White students on the south side of SLPSD attended predominantly White neighborhood schools. When the predominately Black schools were overcrowded, "intact busing" was used as an offsetting strategy. "Intact busing" occurred when Black students and teachers were bused to predominately White schools for teachers to teach and students to learn. These students had different arrival, dismissal, lunch, and recess times than the White students (L. Beckwith, personal communication, December 8, 2016). This system infuriated many Black SLPSD parents, including Minnie Liddell. In 1971, Mrs. Liddell began vocalizing her concerns through various protests.

On February 18, 1972, a class action lawsuit was filed (Liddell v. Board of Education of the City of St. Louis, Missouri) in U.S. District Court, Eastern District of Missouri (Liddell v. Board of Education, 1983). The Board of Education for the City of St. Louis would later file a lawsuit against many suburban school districts located outside of St. Louis City, citing that they also contributed to the segregation in the SLPSD by "assign[ing] and transport[ing] Black students living in the suburbs to Black schools in the city" (Norwood, 2012). Fearful after the presiding district judge threatened to combine and consolidate multiple districts into one metropolitan school district, all parties signed an agreement in 1983 (Norwood, 2012). This agreement gave birth to the voluntary inter-district transfer program. Implemented during the 1983 - 1984 school year, the major components of this agreement included Black students from the city transferring to suburban schools, the creation and growth of magnet schools in the city, and quality educational improvements for the remaining SLPSD students (Norwood, 2012). In 1999, the voluntary inter-district transfer program peaked, with over 14,000 students being transferred from St. Louis City schools (Glaser, n.d.). This same year, an updated Settlement Agreement identified the end of the 2008 - 2009 school year as the final year that the State of Missouri would be obligated to fund the voluntary inter-district transfer program (Norwood, 2012). To say this would mark the end of students from a predominantly Black St. Louis school district transferring to another "high-quality" school district would be premature and eventually proven false.

Section 167.131 of the Outstanding Schools Act (1993) states that an unaccredited district must pay the tuition and transportation cost for each student who attends an accredited school in the same or adjoining district. The Missouri Department of Elementary and Secondary Education (DESE) used performance standards to classify school districts as accredited with distinction, fully accredited, provisionally accredited, or unaccredited (DESE, n.d.). In May 2007, the SLPSD lost its accreditation ("Court upholds decision to rescind St. Louis Public School's accreditation." 2008). Up until this point, St. Louis City residents Jane Turner, Susan Bruker, Gina Breitenfeld, and William Drendel all paid tuition for their children to attend the nearby School District of Clayton (Clayton), which is in St. Louis County (Norwood, 2012). Aware of Missouri Statue 167.131, these same parents requested Clayton to seek reimbursement for tuition from the unaccredited SLPSD (Turner v. School District of Clayton, 2007). When Clayton refused, a lawsuit was filed in St. Louis County Circuit Court (Turner v. School District of Clayton, 2007). Although the Circuit Court sided with Clayton, upon appeal, the Missouri Supreme Court reversed the decision in 2010 and remanded the case back to the St. Louis County Circuit Court (Norwood, 2012). After Clayton argued that the Missouri Supreme Court ruling was unconstitutional and the St. Louis County Court agreed, the case was sent back to the Missouri Supreme Court (Norwood, 2012). By now, Jane Turner, Susan Bruker, and William Drendel were no longer plaintiffs, resulting in the case being renamed [Gina] Breitenfeld v. School District of Clayton (2013).

On June 11, 2013, the Missouri Supreme Court reaffirmed its 2010 decision, ruling that students in unaccredited school districts could transfer to an accredited school district at the expense of the unaccredited district (Breitenfeld v. School District of Clayton, 2013). This ruling would eventually be the impetus for implementing the Student Transfer Program. In 2012, SLPSD was reclassified as provisionally accredited (Bock, 2012.). Being provisionally accredited meant that the 2013 ruling no longer had immediate ramifications for SLPSD; the same could not be said for the Riverview Gardens School District (RGSD).

Unaccredited since 2007, RGSD was one of three unaccredited districts in the state of Missouri in 2013 (Kansas City Public School District & Normandy School District were the other two) (DESE, n.d.). With nearly 6,000 students (96.9% Black) and recent financial struggles, RGSD began implementing the Student Transfer Program precisely thirty years after the voluntary inter-district transfer program started. Only this time, the funding source would not be the State of Missouri; it would be the unaccredited school district. At an estimated 30 million dollars per school year in total cost, the Student Transfer Program was viewed as a bankruptcy program waiting to happen (Salter, J. & Hollingsworth, H. 2013).

Separate but Equal

Education, segregation, and the United States judicial system have been intertwined for over 150 years. In 1850, Sarah Roberts, a five-year-old Black student, attempted to attend an all-White school closer to her Boston, Massachusetts home instead of the less-resourced, all-Black school (Sumner, 1849). When she was not allowed to attend school because of her race, her father, Benjamin Roberts, filed a discrimination suit.
Judge Lemuel Shaw presided over the case and ruled in favor of the City of Boston (Roberts v. City of Boston, 1850). Notwithstanding, in 1855, Massachusetts became the first state to prohibit racially segregated schools in the United States (Desegregating Public Schools, 1855).

In 1896, Plessy v. Ferguson represented the nation's highest legal sanction for the physical separation by race of persons in the United States (Davis, 2004). Homer Adolph Plessy, seven-eighths White and one-eighth Black, boarded a train in Louisiana and sat in a car reserved for white passengers (Medley, 2003). When asked if he was a colored man, Plessy's response resulted in an order to move to a car reserved for African Americans (Medley, 2003). Refusing to comply, Plessy was arrested and later tried in US District Court. Judge John H. Ferguson found that requiring Plessy to move based entirely on his race did not violate the Thirteenth or Fourteenth Amendments (Plessy v. Ferguson, 1896). The US Supreme Court's decision to uphold this ruling confirmed the *Separate but Equal* doctrine, making segregation legal for fifty-eight more years.

In 1951, a class action lawsuit was filed in Topeka, Kansas, challenging the Board of Education's policy on racial segregation in public education. The National Association for the Advancement of Colored People (NAACP) would lead the case in Supreme Court, combining five different cases from Kansas, Delaware, South Carolina, Virginia, and Washington DC that challenged racial segregation in schools (Brown v. Board of Education, 1954).

On May 17, 1954, Brown v. Board of Education of Topeka, Kansas, was decided. The US Supreme Court ruled that the "separate but equal" doctrine adopted in Plessy v. Ferguson, 163 US 537, had no place in public education (Brown v. Board of Education, 1954). The court also stated that "segregation of children in public schools solely based on race deprives children of the minority group of equal educational opportunities, even though the physical facilities and other 'tangible' factors may be equal" (Brown v. Board of Education, 1954).

Although the Brown v. Board of Education decision was considered a victory for racial equality in education, starting court-imposed racial desegregation in schools would take decades for some states. In Brown v. Board of Education II, the courts called for states to desegregate "with all deliberate speed" (1955). The impact of the contrasting words "deliberate" and "speed" allowed some states to move rather slowly, enabling segregation to continue for many more years after Brown II (L. Beckwith, personal communication, December 8, 2016). It would take more court cases and Supreme Court rulings to expedite school desegregation.

In 1971, the Charlotte-Mecklenburg Schools in North Carolina were still considered racially imbalanced. With over 84,000 students (29% Black) and 107 schools, Charlotte-Mecklenburg Schools was considered an enormous school district (Swann v. Charlotte-Mecklenburg Board of Education, 1971). Two-thirds of the 21,000 Black students were attending schools that were 99% Black (Swann v. Charlotte-Mecklenburg Board of Education, 1971). During this time, many states and districts interpreted the Brown rulings as prohibiting segregation, not necessarily as integration mandates. This notion would change (in part) with Swann v. Charlotte-Mecklenburg Board of Education (1971). The US Supreme Court upheld the decision that bus transportation could be used to accomplish school desegregation (Swann v. Charlotte-Mecklenburg Board of Education, 1971). This decision not only articulated the Supreme Court's stance on ensuring equal educational opportunities for all students regardless of race but also opened the door for other states to use buses as a school desegregation strategy (Schwartz, 1986).

At the same time, Swann and the Charlotte-Mecklenburg Schools were battling in court; a similar court battle occurred in Indianapolis, Indiana. In 1971, the Indianapolis Public Schools (IPS) were found guilty of "de jure segregation" for their utilization of gerrymandering attendance boundaries, establishing free transfer zones, and promoting faculty segregation (United States District Court vs. Indianapolis Public Schools, 1975). In this lawsuit, filed by the US Justice Department, the court found that IPS was "operating a segregated school system wherein segregation was imposed and enforced by operation of laws" (United States District Court vs. Indianapolis Public Schools, 1975). Two years later, IPS was ordered to bus "a certain percentage" of their Black students to surrounding schools outside of IPS (Indianapolis Public Schools and Township Schools Busing Agreement, 1998).

Swann v. Charlotte-Mecklenburg and the United States District Court v. Indianapolis Public Schools used busing to desegregate racially segregated school systems. This same strategy would be used repeatedly to provide "equitable quality education." Before we can examine the effectiveness of this strategy, it is vital to understand what constitutes an "equitable quality education" and the mitigating factors.

Equitable Quality Education

In 1965, President Lyndon B. Johnson signed the Elementary and Secondary Education Act. This law was enacted to provide "equitable educational opportunities" to help "enhance the learning experiences of underprivileged children" (Thomas &

Brady, 2005). This meant the federal government would play a role in ensuring equitable and quality education for all students. However, what exactly constitutes equity and quality in education? According to the United States Office of Education, the usage of terms such as "equity" and "quality" are frequently "imprecise and inconsistent" (Improving Education Quality Project, 1993). "Equity," as a stand-alone word in education, is defined as "fairness between distinguishable groups in terms of access to, participation in, and achievement of the educational system" (Cobbe, 1990).

"Quality," on the other hand, typically represents the "degree to which objectives are met, accomplished, or [are] effective" (Improving Education Quality Project, 1993). Together, "equitable [quality] education" represents a "systematic, sustained effort aimed at chang[ing] learning conditions, with the ultimate aim of accomplishing educational goals more effectively" (Bollen, 1989). In my 2021 book, *How to Achieve Educational Equity*, I define educational equity as "creating and or eliminating policies systems and practices in schools that impact the experiences, outcomes, and access to resources for students from previously excluded groups."

When considering learning conditions for students, one must understand the contrast between Black and White schools. The *Equality of Educational Opportunity Report* (1966) proved that students' backgrounds and socioeconomic status impact their learning conditions. Schools serving Black students, especially those in the inner-city, often face the challenges associated with disadvantaged neighborhoods (Jacobs, 2007), most notably poverty. The research is clear; there is a substantial relationship between poverty and student achievement; "[a]s the percent of poverty increases in a school, student achievement goes down" (The Relationships Between School Poverty and Student Achievement in Maine, 2014). Across the nation, many of the highest-performing schools are in the wealthiest neighborhoods (Hochschild & Scovronick, 2013). There is such a correlation between student achievement and zip codes that the quality of education received is "entirely predictable, based on where you live" (Domenech, 2011). It may be safe to state that such a notion provides a solid argument for those who believe that students who live in poverty, but attend schools in "rich" neighborhoods, should perform better than those who remain in poverty-stricken neighborhoods. The keyword here undoubtedly is "should."

The Use of Busing to Achieve Equity

Desegregation was believed to be a way for Black students to increase their educational achievement by accessing significantly more educational resources, which were prevalent in "White schools" (Flentroy, 1977). In 1955, social scientist Gordon Allport stated that the greater the contact between races, the greater the chances for "mutual understanding and tolerance of cultural differences." According to Glynda Flentroy (1977):

> *[T]here have been four distinct factors motivating school integration: (1) the removal of the Black inferiority stigma in order to heighten [self-esteem], (2) access by Black*

20

pupils to superior resources at White institutions, (3) increasing the academic achievement of Black students, and (4) lessening racial prejudice. Among the factors motivating school integration, the scholastic performance of Black students in an integrated academic environment has received the most attention from social scientists.

Based on the noted benefits of integration, why are buses necessary to achieve school integration? An explanation that has been provided so often focuses on de jure segregation, de facto segregation, and "White flight."

De jure segregation is defined as "legally keeping society separated by the creation of laws and statutes that restrict or make it impossible for minority citizens to exercise their rights" (Grace, 2014). Contrarily, de facto segregation is a non-government-mandated segregation in which events outside governmental control result in a segregated society (Grace, 2014). "White flight" refers to the relocation of Whites to the suburbs as a direct result of Blacks migrating to the central cities where Whites reside (Boustan, 2010). When considering the impact that de jure segregation, de facto segregation, and "White flight" had on historically segregated states, cities, and school districts, "busing" became a viable option for achieving integration. One of those historically segregated states was Missouri.

As previously stated, Missouri was admitted as a slave state to the Union through the Missouri Compromise (1820), which represented the northernmost state requiring separate schools for Whites and Blacks (Gotham, 2002). In 1910, the Missouri State Attorney General informed all Missouri school districts that the state would prosecute any school officials operating racially integrated schools (Gotham, 2002). In addition to schools being segregated, Shelley v. Kraemer would serve as an example of how neighborhoods in Missouri were just as segregated as the schools.

In 1945, a Black family moved into an overwhelmingly White St. Louis, Missouri, neighborhood. Unbeknownst to this family, their new home, just north of the 4600 block of St. Louis Ave. in the Greater Ville area, had a restrictive covenant that prevented Blacks from moving into the property (Shelley v. Kraemer, 1948). The United States Supreme Court would overturn the lower court's decision that housing covenants were constitutional, ruling that "racially restrictive covenants violated the United States Constitution" (Shelley v. Kraemer, 1948). The state of race relations during this time would lead to the "most widespread outbreak of racial violence in the city's post-World War II history" (O'Connor, 2009).

On June 21, 1949, the Fairgrounds Park riot would occur less than two miles from the Shelley's home on the first day that the previously all-White Fairgrounds Park pool was racially integrated (O'Conner, 2009). Thousands of White youths brandished bats, clubs, sticks, and knives, striking many unsuspecting victims

(O'Conner, 2009). It would take more than 400 police officers and 12 hours to restore order (O'Conner, 2009).

Given Missouri's large number of racially segregated schools and communities following the Brown I ruling, "busing" would become one of the most frequently used options to comply with the Brown II ruling.

The Kirkwood R-VII School District is located in the suburbs of St. Louis County, Missouri. In 1973, the Office for Civil Rights (OCR) required Kirkwood to explain the "substantial racial disproportion" in their schools (US Commission on Civil Rights, 1977). Kirkwood responded with plans to appoint a "biracial interpersonal relations committee" that would take action to address their racially disproportionate schools by the 1974-75 school year (US Commission on Civil Rights, 1977). Kirkwood's desegregation plan in 1975, which the OCR later accepted, addressed how they would eliminate racial isolation and their traditional dual school system (US Commission on Civil Rights, 1977). In this plan, Kirkwood would close the predominantly Black J. Milton Turner Elementary School and bus students to other predominantly White schools within the district. This infuriated the Black community.

The United States Commission on Civil Rights reported that:

> *The minority community felt that it was assuming an additional burden because its own school was closed and all its children would have to ride the bus. It protested that, aside from the unequal burden, busing presented*

> *particular problems for them since unavoidable tardiness would mean the loss of a day's schooling for their children, while white children would lose only a few hours under similar circumstances. Blacks also perceived [the] Turner School as a vital part of the community. They felt that white students might have been bused into Turner to preserve the school.*

This report also claimed that the desegregation plan used in the Kirkwood R-VII School District was a success (US Commission on Civil Rights, 1977). "The district is working hard to overcome or avoid such problems and ensure that Kirkwood schools are providing quality desegregated education of which the entire community can be proud" (US Commission on Civil Rights, 1977). Approximately fifteen miles down the road, however, there was another community in the City of St. Louis, Missouri, that was not proud of the quality of education that was being provided by their school district.

Glynda Flentroy (1977) listed "access by Black pupils to superior resources at White institutions" as one of the distinct factors motivating school integration; SLPSD parent Minnie Liddell felt the same way. Following the Brown v. Board of Education ruling, St. Louis Public School District schools were still racially segregated. Many of the schools in the southern portion of the district were predominantly White, while schools in the northern portion were predominantly Black (Liddell v. Board of Education, 1972). According to Minnie

24

Liddell, Black students attended old, inferior, overcrowded schools and used the worn-out books that were previously used by the all-White SLPSD schools. In 1972, Mrs. Liddell and a group of concerned parents filed a lawsuit against the Board of Education for the City of St. Louis. The lawsuit aimed to obtain quality education for their Black children (Liddell v. Board of Education, 1972). In 1975, attorneys from both sides entered a Consent Decree that resulted in the SLPSD Board of Education pledging to increase the number of minority teachers and decrease racial imbalances with the creation of programs such as magnet schools (Voluntary Interdistrict Choice Corporation, 2016). The NAACP objected to this settlement and was allowed to intervene in the case due to an overturned decision by the US Circuit Court of Appeals (Voluntary Interdistrict Choice Corporation, 2016).

In 1980, the St. Louis Court of Appeals reversed one of its previous decisions regarding segregated schools in St. Louis (Voluntary Interdistrict Choice Corporation, 2016).

> *[U]ntil 1979, [and] long after the separate but equal doctrine was ruled unconstitutional, the Missouri Constitution contained an article calling for separate schools. The [US Appeals] Court suggests the development of an exchange program between the city and the county and returns the case to Meredith. [Afterwards,] St. Louis school officials submit plans for an intradistrict (within the district) desegregation plan [that is] approved by the [US Appeals] Court for implementation [in] September,*

[1980] with the transfer of 7,500 students within the city district.

After SLPSD filed a lawsuit against 23 St. Louis County school districts, a desegregation plan, including "busing," would be agreed upon in 1983 and implemented at the start of the 1983 - 84 school year. All St. Louis metropolitan school districts accepted this Settlement Agreement (1983) and, according to the Voluntary Interdistrict Choice Corporation (2016), the agreement had:

> *[M]ultiple components, including the transfer of black city students into primarily white suburban districts and white suburban students into magnet schools in the city. Transportation and tuition costs were fully paid by the State of Missouri. The preliminary goal for suburban districts was to reach Plan Ratio (a 15 percent increase of all African-American students in the district including resident students.) The ultimate goal was for districts to achieve the Plan Goal which was a 25 percent black student population.*

This plan would later be known as the "St. Louis Voluntary Inter-District Transfer Program."

The St. Louis Voluntary Inter-District Transfer Program

The St. Louis Voluntary Inter-District Transfer Program was initially overseen by the Voluntary Interdistrict Coordinating Council (VIC), which, in 1999, became a non-profit entity and was renamed the Voluntary Interdistrict Choice Corporation (VICC) (Voluntary Interdistrict Choice Corporation, 2016). In 1983, VIC was granted the task of implementing the inter-district transfer program. The transfer program consisted of (1) transferring 15,000 Black students living in St. Louis City to suburban schools, (2) providing the establishment and growth of magnet schools in the city, and (3) providing quality educational improvements and capital improvements for the estimated 10,000 – 15,000 students who would remain in segregated St. Louis Public Schools (Norwood, 2012). However, these claims and many of Norwood's claims have been questioned by SLPSD employees during this time. Dr. Lynn Beckwith Jr. (2017), who took exception to #3, stated that the State of Missouri and SLPSD were required by the US Court to make these improvements as outlined in the Court-ordered Intradistrict Desegregation Plan.

When the St. Louis Voluntary Inter-District Transfer Program officially started in 1983, it was the most extensive desegregation plan in the entire country (Heaney & Uchitelle, 2004). It was also the only plan 100% funded by the state (Heaney & Uchitelle, 2004). The cost was $75.5 million annually, or $7,257 per pupil (Heaney & Uchitelle, 2004).

Based on a 1993 focus-group study, Dr. Susan Uchitelle reported that most Black students who transferred rated their experiences in the county schools as positive (Heaney & Uchitelle, 2004). It must be noted that these results have been challenged due to Dr. Uchitelle's, who served as VICC's supervisor, vested interest and perceived bias about VICC (L. Beckwith, personal communication, March 22, 2017). This same report reflected overwhelmingly positive sentiments by White students as well. One student admitted that his previous stereotypes were false, stating that he met many "really nice [Black] guys" through sports (Heaney & Uchitelle, 2004).

The inter-district transfer program certainly changed high school sports in St. Louis. According to Steve Warmack, former principal of Roosevelt High School, 90% of St. Louis County's outstanding athletes were transfer students recruited from St. Louis City. A thoughtful analysis of available data lends some validity to Mr. Warmack's claims, at least with respect to the impact transfers had on both St. Louis City and St Louis County. For example, from 1970-1981, the 11 years before the voluntary [inter-district] transfer program, St. Louis County schools won 6 Missouri High School State Championships in basketball, football, and track & field, sports that have been historically dominated by Black student athletes (Fields, 2012). In that same span, St. Louis City schools won 11 Missouri High School State Championships in basketball, football, and track & field (Fields, 2012). From 1982 to 1987, following the implementation of the St. Louis Voluntary Inter-District Transfer Program, St. Louis City schools won 7 Missouri State High

School Championships in basketball, football, and track & field, while the St. Louis County schools that accepted students from St. Louis City via the inter-district transfer program won 8 Missouri State High School Championships (Fields, 2012). In the first year of the inter-district transfer program, approximately 1,327 transfer students from the city participated in extracurricular activities (McKenna & Uchitelle, 1984). By 1987, the number of transfer students from the city who participated in extracurricular activities had increased to approximately 5,516 (Campbell & Uchitelle, 1987). From 1988 - 1999, St. Louis City schools won a total of 6 Missouri State High School Championships in basketball, football, and track & field, while St. Louis County schools that accepted students from St. Louis City won 18 Missouri State High School Championships in basketball, football, and track & field (Fields, 2012). Almost 13,000 transfer students attended school through the transfer program in 1999. Of the 7,683 transfer students who participated in extracurricular activities, 40.9% participated in three or more activities (Fields, 2012). It is important to note that when student-athletes transferred from the city to become student-athletes in the county, the city schools lost out on sports and activity funds generated during sports contests and activities. In many cases, these funds help to offset the lack of adequate school funding.

Academically, it has been much more of a challenge to juxtapose the student performance of those who participated in the St. Louis Voluntary Inter-District Transfer Program with students who remained in SLPSD, as DESE's annual performance reports did not disaggregate data by student transfer status until 2012.

In 1988, then-Governor John Ashcroft revealed that the transfer program was a waste of money, costing the State of Missouri $500 million in only five years of the program (Desegregation Fifth Year, 1988). There was little question that the financial burden of the inter-district transfer program was immense in the eyes of Missouri politicians and policymakers. In 1996, then-Attorney General Jay Nixon filed a motion to terminate the voluntary inter-district transfer program (Heaney & Uchitelle, 2004). He argued that the State of Missouri:

> *[H]ad complied with all prior court orders, had demonstrated its good-faith commitment to desegregate, had eliminated all vestiges of the prior de jure segregation to the extent that was practical, and had proposed a transition plan that provided enough money for the St. Louis [Public] School District to make the transition from a school district undergoing desegregation to a unitary district. The state said it had spent $1.834 billion between 1980 and 1996, or $115 million per year. Of that sum, $1,300 per pupil was for transportation costs, and the remainder of $4,700 per pupil was the payment to the receiving schools for the full cost of educating the transfer student.*

The United States argued that the burden was on the state to show that the city school system had achieved unitary (forming a single, non-segregated entity) status (Heaney & Uchitelle, 2004). In 1997, Attorney General Nixon requested an order to relieve the State of Missouri for paying for this transfer program, stating that Missouri had "done its share;" the Eighth Circuit Court agreed (Heaney & Uchitelle, 2004). In 1998, the Missouri General Assembly passed Senate Bill 781, which laid the foundation for an official settlement agreement to end the voluntary transfer program (Heaney & Uchitelle, 2004). In 1999, a new Settlement Agreement marked the end of the 2008 – 2009 school year as the last year for the State of Missouri to fund the St. Louis Voluntary Inter-District Transfer Program (VICC, 2016). The 1999 Settlement Agreement also included a separate agreement with participating school districts that allowed for a ten-year maximum extension (Norwood, 2012). As of 2016, 4,300 students from the city were attending suburban school districts through VICC and 140 county students were attending city magnet schools (VICC, 2016). The current provision of the 1999 Settlement Agreement enables VICC to accept students in the voluntary inter-district transfer program through the 2023 – 2024 school year. There will be no new students enrolled in the voluntary inter-district transfer program during the 2024-2025 school year or beyond (VICC, 2023).

The "New" Inter-district Transfer Program

When the Outstanding Schools Act of 1993 (SB 380) was signed into law by then-Governor Mel Carnahan, it was believed that it would help Missouri create a state-wide educational system that would be "second to none" (Outstanding Schools Act of 1993). Under this act, all Missouri students were provided a better opportunity for a quality educational experience, regardless of where they lived (Outstanding Schools

Act of 1993). This statement was made possible, in part, due to the heavier accountability measures that were embedded into the Outstanding Schools Act, particularly section 167.131. In this section:

> *[t]he board of education of each district in this state that does not maintain an accredited school pursuant to the authority of the state board of education to classify schools as established in section 161.092 shall pay the tuition of and provide transportation consistent with the provisions of section 167.241 for each pupil resident therein who attends an accredited school in another district of the same or an adjoining county.*

In 2007, St. Louis Public School District lost its accreditation. That same year, a group of parents who resided in SLPSD and, up to this point, were paying for their children to attend the nearby School District of Clayton sued because of section 167.131. They argued that since SLPSD was unaccredited, the School District of Clayton should bill SLPSD for their children's tuition (Turner v. School District of Clayton, 2007).

The court would reach a ruling in this case on June 11, 2013 (Breitenfeld v. School District of Clayton, 2013). By this time, SLPSD was no longer unaccredited. However, approximately 10 miles north, the Riverview Gardens School District was one of two unaccredited North St. Louis County school districts; Normandy School District was the other (Kansas City Public Schools was the third unaccredited school district in the state of Missouri as of June 2013). Unaccredited since 2007, Riverview Gardens began implementing the Student Transfer Program right after this ruling. Although the Outstanding Schools Act required unaccredited school districts to pay for the tuition and provide transportation for any student who decided to attend an accredited district, DESE required Riverview Gardens to provide transportation to only two districts (L. Beckwith, personal communication, March 22, 2017). Therefore, Riverview Gardens decided to pay the transportation cost (and tuition) for students transferring to the Kirkwood School District and the Mehlville School District. This decision was made, in part, due to Kirkwood and Mehlville's 2013 tuition being commensurate to the tuition in Riverview Gardens (L. Beckwith, personal communication, March 22, 2017). Eventually, Riverview would send thousands of students to schools outside their school district. The Kirkwood School District office was nearly 27 miles from the Riverview Gardens School District office and the Mehlville School District office was nearly 24 miles from the Riverview Gardens School District office. Both Kirkwood and Mehlville are well over an hour round trip commute.

During the first four years of the Student Transfer Program, 2,680 Riverview Gardens students participated. 1,063 students during the 2013 – 2014 school year, 717 students during the 2014 – 2015 school year, 520 students during 2015 – 2016, and 437 students during the 2016 – 2017 school year (L. Beckwith, personal communication, December 10, 2016). The newest Missouri Student Transfer Program was well underway.

Missouri's Accreditation System

As of January 1, 2016, Riverview Gardens and Normandy were the only two school districts in Missouri without some level of accreditation status (DESE, n.d.). Both districts' demographic data showed that they were predominantly Black and that more than 90% of their total enrollment qualified for free or reduced lunch (DESE, n.d.). In 2012, St. Louis Public School District and Kansas City Public School District were both unaccredited ("So You've Lost Accreditation, What Now? A How-To, How-Not-To Guide from Kansas City and St. Louis - NextSTL." 2012). They were also both predominantly Black, with nearly 90% of their total enrollment qualifying for free or reduced lunch (DESE, n.d.). In addition to demographics, these districts had also shown similar school performance (DESE, n.d.).

During the 2016-2017 school year, public schools and districts in Missouri were accredited using the fifth cycle of the Missouri School Improvement Program (MSIP5).

Updated in July 2014, this statewide public school accountability measure outlined student achievement expectations and college and career readiness criteria. MSIP5 computed an Annual Performance Report (APR) to promote growth based on the performance standards - Academic Achievement, Subgroup Achievement, High School Readiness or College and Career Readiness, Attendance Rate, and Graduation Rate (DESE, 2014). Data from the APR was then used to determine the accreditation level of a school or district. The four MSIP5 accreditation levels were

Accredited with Distinction, Accredited, Provisionally Accredited, and Unaccredited (DESE, 2014). The maximum points that a K-12 district could obtain was one hundred and forty (140). In theory, one hundred and twenty-six (126) points would be needed to score in the Accredited with Distinction range, ninety-eight (98) points would be needed to score in the Accredited range, seventy (70) points would be needed to score in the Provisionally Accredited range, and fewer than seventy (70) points resulted in the Unaccredited range (DESE, 2014). Although a district could score in a particular range, accreditation classification recommendations were made based on APR statuses and trends and presented to the Missouri State Board of Education for final determination (DESE, 2014).

Despite implementing the Student Transfer Program, the Riverview Gardens School District has made tremendous performance improvements, as measured by their APR. In 2013, the Riverview Gardens Special Administrative Board appointed a new superintendent, Dr. Scott Spurgeon, who led the district to subsequent APR increases.

Riverview Gardens received forty (40) points out of one hundred and forty points (140), or twenty- eight percent (28.6%) in 2013 (DESE, n.d.). After the first year of the Student Transfer Program, Riverview Gardens received sixty-three and a half (63.5) points out of one hundred and forty points (140), or forty-five percent (45.4%) (DESE, n.d.). In 2015, one hundred and eleven points (111) points, or seventy-nine-point three percent (79.3%), were received (DESE, n.d.). In 2016, Riverview Gardens received one hundred and four point five points (104.5) points, or seventy-four-point six percent (74.6%) (DESE, n.d.). Due to the noted progress, the Riverview Gardens School District requested an accreditation classification upgrade. While awaiting a ruling on the accreditation classification upgrade, the Riverview Gardens Special Administrative Board was required by DESE to adopt a Student Transfer Transition Plan and Memorandum of Understanding, with all accredited school districts who participated in the Student Transfer Program, as a precursor for recommending any accreditation upgrade to the State Board of Education (L. Beckwith, personal communication, March 22, 2017).

On December 2, 2016, the Missouri Board of Education voted to upgrade the Riverview Gardens School District from Unaccredited to Provisionally Accredited. Riverview Gardens became Provisionally Accredited effective January 4, 2017. The previously referenced Transition Plan and Memorandum of Understanding with the 22 receiving districts allowed the Student Transfer Program to continue after the 2016 – 2017 school year. Under this plan, qualified students were authorized to continue to enroll in and attend school within the Receiving District for three (3) subsequent academic school years or until the student reached a natural shift to the next grade span (i.e., moving from elementary school to middle school or from middle school to high school), whichever timeline is shorter (Reference MOU).

Case Study

The Riverview Gardens School District is located in North St. Louis County, Missouri. According to the Missouri Census Data Center (2016), in 2010, the Riverview Gardens attendance area had a total population of 41,192. The district covers nine square miles, with a population density of 4,382 per square mile. Homeowners comprised 59.4% of the population, while the remaining 40.6% were renters. Of the 16,599 total housing units within the Riverview Gardens School District, 12.7% were listed as vacant, according to the 2010 census.

This 2017 case study collected data at undisclosed locations within the Riverview Gardens School District. These locations were carefully identified as calm, quiet, and free from high levels of distraction, making them ideal for conducting personal interviews.

Discussions With Families

Three specific participants were selected to be interviewed in this case study due to their similar, yet unique first-hand experiences and perspectives related to the Student Transfer Program. The participants were all women aged 39 to 48. All interviews lasted approximately 60 minutes using an established interview protocol. To protect the identity of the participants, the following pseudonyms were used as individual identifiers:

(Participant 1) Jennifer - The mother of three students enrolled in Riverview Gardens. She decided to keep her children in the district despite having the Student Transfer Program as an option to attend a nearby accredited district.

(Participant 2) Michelle - Mother of two students enrolled in a nearby accredited school district (Kirkwood School District) via the Student Transfer Program. Both students attended Riverview Gardens before transferring to Kirkwood.

(Participant 3) Tiffany - Mother of three students who were enrolled in Riverview Gardens. She transferred her children to a nearby accredited district (Kirkwood School District) via the Student Transfer Program. She decided to transfer her children back to Riverview Gardens five months into the program.

Jennifer's Interview (Conducted in 2017)

(HF= Howard Fields /J= Jennifer)

>HF: *Without using individual names, can you talk about each of your school-aged children?*
>
>J: *Okay, so, I have three sons. Um. Freshman, Junior and a 7th grader. Um. They are all very energetic. Two of them are really eager to learn. They are all athletic. And they all have something special and genuine to bring to the table, um, as far as their personalities, their demeanors. Their needs and wants are very different, but yet similar in some ways.*
>
>HF: *In 2013, a judge ruled that students in unaccredited school districts were eligible to*

transfer to an accredited school district via the Student Transfer Law. What were your initial views regarding this ruling?

J: *Actually, I transferred my children INTO the Riverview Gardens School District right after that ruling. Uh, my babies were in private school, and so the school was closing down and we had a choice to transfer them to a sister school or bring them to Riverview Gardens, because we lived in the district, and my husband and I decided that they would come into the Riverview Gardens School District.*

HF: *What were your school-aged children's views regarding this ruling?*

J: *Um, my oldest, [who was a junior in high school at the time of the interview], was the only one that had some questions, because he is...being the oldest, he kind of had heard what the community was saying, and what a lot of the other children were saying, but he really didn't,... it didn't bother him too much. He still came in and was treated pretty much the same as he was, maybe actually a little bit better than the private school which he came from, so it didn't have a major impact on them at all.*

HF: *Okay. You said that he had a few questions. Can you give me an example of some of those questions or some of the things he heard from the community?*

J: *Well, one of the questions was why would I take them out of a private school and take them*

39

into a school that was a failing district. And where did he get that from? Well, the media has a way of painting a picture that is not great at all. And he's a child, so he's going to go off what he's hearing. And then some of the kids that were already in the district, I guess, um, was telling him that they were unaccredited, trying to tell him what that meant, but he wasn't getting the correct answers until he decided to come home and ask.

HF: *To the best of your knowledge, how did your family's views regarding the Student Transfer Program compare to the views of other family members within your community?*

J: *Well, I didn't agree with the transfer program. I didn't agree with it, and I didn't like the program that they were offering the program.*

HF: *What didn't you like about it?*

J: *Well...those are the same families that got the district to where they were. Those families should have been made to remain and help get the district back to where it needed to be. The district didn't lose their accreditation because of some outside person. These people were here. When the accreditation was lost, they should have come together: town hall meetings or whatever, however, to work out a game plan, to assist the district in getting back its accreditation.*

HF: *What led to your initial decision to transfer your children into Riverview Gardens? Let me rephrase that question because you have a unique situation, you transferred them in. What led to your initial decision to not transfer your students to a different district that was being offered as a byproduct of the Student Transfer Program?*

J: *Well, one thing was, when we found out the private school our children were in was closing down, and we would have to go to another school, we had to kind of do our research on Riverview Gardens School District ourselves. Um, and, if the private school can close, and this district is still here but they're still fighting and trying, we wanted to give that same opportunity to our children, like we gave the private school an [opportunity], a chance, and it didn't work out. So, we came into Riverview Gardens, and it has actually been a very good experience for all of my kids.*

HF: *You say "a really good experience". Can you speak to that?*

J: *Um, sure. So, my oldest one, he made some decisions and, um, choices that were not the best for him, but it was not because of the schooling. My middle son is soaring greatly as a freshman. Um, he has, when he went to do his shadow days, when he goes out into different colleges to do different visits or whatever, a lot of things that he is hearing or seeing, he learned that from the middle school, where he attained his 6th, 7th, and 8th grade education. Um, he sees some things that he was taught in Riverview Gardens School District as a young child. Now that he is a freshman, he considers himself a young man, Um, he's able to compare some of those things. My youngest son has been doing great. Like, he has not missed a beat. Um, He came into Riverview Gardens School District reading well below level, and Um, once he got into the district, the principal he had at that time had him tested, had his dad and I take him through some different programs or whatever and we just found out he wasn't being challenged or being made to do anything different at his private school that he was attending. Um, that was very costly. So, he continued on with these different programs, different testing, different programs, different testing and now he's above where he should be and he's, you know, doing very well academically.*

HF: *What impact did your decision to stay in the Riverview Gardens School District have as a parent socially, with other parents?*

J: *Well, because I'm new to the district, as a new parent, there were parents that were able to tell me their opinion of Riverview Gardens School District. And, of course, teeth and tongue fall out, so I was able to be that... Well, did you try this? Did you do that? Well, naw, I did such and such and such and such. Well, you know, you can't always bail out. Because if you don't want to find out what the problem is, you just want to run, that doesn't teach your child anything. And so, for us, it was really challenging because we were bringing our children into the district, while some of our family and friends were taking their children out of the district. Um, now they see where our kids are, some of them have brought their children back, and have discussed bringing their children back next year. My thing is, you know, you're still rocking the boat.*

HF: *Um, a lot of times, you said you were new to the district, so they (they being the other parents) would give their other opinions. I'm interested to know, were the opinions based on academics, discipline, combination of all...what were their opinions specifically about Riverview Gardens?*

J: *It was a combination of...you know, everyone has an opinion, but their opinions were based off basically, their lack of knowledge. So, when you as a parent don't attend parent-teacher conference, you don't answer your phone when the school is calling, you don't go to the school just periodically to find out what's going on in the district, or what happened that [got us] here, you tend to just get on the bandwagon with the other complaining parents or naysayers. So, for me it was the thing of, you know, being new in the district, um, we listened to the news, we watched the news, but we were those parents that did further research. Why did the district lose its accreditation? Why is it such a high turnover? But when you look at Riverview Gardens turnover, it's no different than any other school district's staff turnover, be it private school, charter school, anything. And, for myself, I was an educator in the charter school, but my kids attended private school. So, it was a lot of having to do a lot of research and listening and just kind of making our own final decision on what we were gonna do with the boys.*

HF: *What impact did your decision not to exercise your right to go to another district have on your school-aged children, socially?*

J: *None. They did not miss a beat.*

HF: *And what was that evidenced by? Just their conversations with you, or...?*

J: *They never asked to leave the school, they never asked could they transfer, could they go with their friends, could they go back to their old school, and that was the only concern that I did have, is, how would I respond if they asked, but I never got that question, so...*

HF: *Thank you. What impact did your decision to transfer have on you as a parent, I'm sorry, What impact did your decision NOT to transfer have on you as a parent emotionally?*

J: *It had no impact. I'm a very involved parent. I was always, if I got a call about grades, if I got a call about behavior, whatever the school* contacted me about via one-on-one with the principal, a teacher, school reach, I made sure that I attended whatever meetings and appointments that were made available by the district.

HF: *What impact did your decision not to transfer have on your school-aged children emotionally?*

J: *None.*

HF: *What impact did your decision not to transfer have on your school-aged children academically?*

J: *It had, well, two of my babies, two of my sons, they actually did better once they transferred into the school district. My other son, he was already, you know, just, he doesn't like school. So, he just did what he had to do to get by. But two of them really excelled a great deal.*

HF: *When you say they did better, what was that evidenced by?*

J: *Their grades, their behaviors, um, willingness to learn, studying more, reading more. They just did a lot better once they got into the district.*

HF: *Were there any unforeseen challenges that your family experienced as a result of not transferring? If so, what were they?*

J: *We didn't have any.*

HF: *As you reflect on your decision not to transfer, as well as everything we have discussed so far, would you have changed any of your previous decisions regarding the Student Transfer Program? Why or why not?*

J: No. Um, they weren't a part of the district losing their accreditation, but I feel like they were a part of it being given back. Um, my kids have done very well, They've not had any issues with teachers, they've not had any issues with peers. They've just done very well academically, um, behaviorally, socially. Um, and then again, as a parent, you have to be involved, and ask questions, and not go off of what everyone else is saying, or the media.

HF: *What are your views on Riverview Gardens regaining provisional accreditation on January the 4th, 2017, thus ending the Student Transfer Program in its current form?*

J: So, I haven't really done a lot of studying on the transfer program, but I...I'm trying to say it right. I think if the children are going to come back...it shouldn't be that they can come back and then start issues or problems. Or the parents and families shouldn't be able to come in and then tear up what you all here have worked so hard to get. If that makes sense. Because the teachers have worked really hard. Dr. Spurgeon has worked extremely hard. So, to get your team together to build this far, which I think it should have been more than just provisional [accreditation], but to allow those families back...I just think it should be not just, you can just walk back in the door.

HF: *Based on your response, what problems do you think could arise, as a result of the district receiving provisional accreditation?*

J: *It's great that we, that the district has it back, but then if you bring children back in the district, who are not going to school on a day-to-day basis where they are, having behavior issues in the district that they are currently attending, or they're not coming to school on a day-to-day basis, then that's going to come and fall right back into the dis[trict]...the Riverview Gardens School District and put us right back where [we] started. So, I think it's just...I don't really know how to say it, but it's kind of a catch-22 I guess.*

HF: *What are your school-aged children's views on Riverview Gardens regaining provisionally accreditation on January the 4th?*

J: *Well, my 7th grade son, because he doesn't really understand the whole gamut, he wants to know why did it take so long, and why only provisional. Um, so I've explained it to him as best that I can and um, and I've taken him to a couple meetings with me. I've had him look online, kind of reading some things. But it is still a lot for a 13-year-old to process, so he's still trying to understand it. Um, the other two feel like, um, can't say the terms, but they feel like the state wants to play games with us because we are predominately African American school[s]. That's the best way I can say it.*

Considering they're older and they clearly know what has happened.

HF: *You said the state wanted to play games because we're an African American school. Can you speak a little bit in terms of if people don't necessarily know St. Louis, or don't know, can you...because this may be [studied] in, you know, different cities, whatever. Can you speak a little bit to that?*

J: *So, if you do the research in any of the 9 elementary schools Riverview Gardens have, the one high school, the two middle schools. So, if you check the demographics, it's predominately all minority, African American students. You can count the number of any other nationality of children that attend the district. So, in my children's eyes, and they coming from a private school, where they were 3 [Black students] in the entire school. They were 3 of the 50 children that made up the school of 585 children when they were closing the building. So, they have family in various school districts, so they know, like I said, the two older ones, know, they understand, and they see more, and they can have a conversation with me about when you're a predominately Black school, when you're a predominately White school, what's the difference, you know. And they just feel, and that was their opinion, their words, because I hadn't even looked at it that way, but they just feel like, momma, is it because we are a predominately Black district, that they [are]*

48

playing yo-yo, is what my oldest son said, with the kids that are in the Riverview Gardens School District. Um, he's trying to figure out why is it Riverview Gardens outscored and out tested other districts around us, but they still have full accreditation, and Riverview Gardens doesn't have it.

HF: *You said that there were some difference between, um, Black schools and White schools, what's one or a few differences that they would [see], coming from their eyes, from the students' perspective?*

J: *One of the things they've said is, they have friends that, like I said, attend districts all over, um, and for my 9th grade son, his view is kind of like one of those, old type thoughts, his thing is, you know, we already are several steps behind everyone else, but why is it those that are already behind, they're never acknowledged, you never hear about them, they're always put in the limelight, they're the ones who you always see on the sports something with the news, or whatever, I don't look at it. But whatever the sports part is on the news. But you don't see Riverview Gardens. So, I didn't have an answer, because, like I said, I don't look at the sports part of the news, so I didn't even really know too much [of] what he was talking about. For my oldest son, his thing is, well, momma, is it that because we're always doing things this way, or we're expected to do things this way, is that why we're always on the news, versus, um, schools that really, just like, right across the bridge, have issues and things going on, but you don't hear about it. Schools right here in their back door have a lot of things going on, but you don't hear it. You always hear Riverview Gardens. So, I had to explain it as best as I felt for them to hear it, you know, that's more for you all to go to school and do better, to show those people that just because I'm, the color of my skin, does not denominate, does not say that I'm less a person or that my district is less a district, you know, because of our skin tone.*

HF: *One of the rationales behind the implementation of the Student Transfer Program is to ensure that all students have access to a quality and equitable education. What does that mean to you?*

J: *Well, I wonder what they mean when they say that. Because you don't see them in anybody's classroom, walking down any halls of any school. You're not coming in to help. So, instead of tearing down, come in and see what you can do to help. Teachers have it hard. They have...principals have it hard, but if you just want to keep sitting on the back burner, and you just want to keep lighting that fire even more, instead of coming in and seeing what's going on, or how you can lend a helping hand, for me, that really shouldn't even be stated. What is a quality education? They, they keep saying that and throwing that term around, but have yet to say what that really means or what that's supposed to look like.*

HF: *Based on your family's experience with the Student Transfer Program, do you believe this program creates opportunities for all students to receive access to a quality and equitable education? Why or why not?*

J: *I say no. Because a lot of the districts, I feel like they took the kids in because it was a dollar, and it was a way for them to build up their schools and increase their finances. I don't think a lot of the districts that took our children really wanted our babies out there, they just took 'em.*

HF: *What is your biggest takeaway from the Student Transfer Program?*

J: *What did we really teach our children?*

HF: *Expand on that a little bit.*

J: *Because the ship is sinking does that mean you just abandon the ship, or do you figure out how you can do, what you can do to get the ship back up like it's supposed to be. It didn't send a good message to me. But you can still live here, but you can't be educated here. That, that...*

HF: *Is there any question you wished I would have asked you or anything you would like to speak to that was not necessarily conveyed in this formal interview?*

J: *Not that I can think of, no.*

HF: *Okay. Well, again, thank you so much.*

Michelle's Interview (Conducted in 2017)

(HF= Howard Fields/M= Michelle)

HF: *Without using individual names, can you talk about each of your school-aged children?*

M: *Well, my oldest one graduated from high school last year, and my middle son is now a freshman in high school. He graduated 8th grade last school year.*

HF: *In 2013, a judge ruled that students in unaccredited school districts were eligible to transfer to an accredited school district via the Student Transfer Law. What were your initial views regarding this ruling?*

M: *My initial views were mixed a little bit because I was confused about it. But once I understood what it was all about, I still thought about; should I have my kids leave their home district. How would they feel with going to a new school with new kids, all that stuff. And I sat and talked with them, and they were like, "mom, let's do this."*

HF: *What were your school-aged children's views on the ruling and them potentially going to another school?*

M: *They...pretty much almost the same thing. You know, they wanted a good education, and you know, they relied on me to help them through that process, 'cause they didn't know if they stayed with Riverview, if Riverview became accredited, or if they didn't, what would that mean when they graduated. They weren't sure. So, they just, you know, we talked, and that's what happened.*

HF: *To the best of your knowledge, how did your family views regarding the Student Transfer Program compare to the views of other family members or other people in your community?*

M: *Um...we had mixed feelings. Some family were like, "why would you leave the district, you've had them there since kindergarten." And some were like, just like with me, education. Education comes first, and that's not saying that Riverview wouldn't have had that education, but I didn't know.*

HF: *What led to your initial decision to transfer?*

M: *Education. I wanted my kids to have a fighting chance.*

HF: *What type of education were they having in Riverview?*

M: *They were having...it's hard to explain. Like, when my middle, or I'm sorry, my older son left the district before the transfer program, he was having issues with the middle school. So, he left before the transfer program. And the teacher that he had was a good teacher, but the students*

53

that were in the class, I just, I couldn't...at the end of the school year, my son was sitting outside of the classroom being taught, as opposed to being taught inside of the classroom. And, as far as my middle son, he was still in elementary school, and the elementary school that he was at, I loved. He loved. He loved the teachers, he was doing class work a year...what's the word I'm looking for...like if he was in 3rd grade he was doing 4th grade work, in 4th grade he was doing 5th grade work, and so on and so forth. So, elementary school was great, middle school, I just, I just couldn't do.

HF: *What impact did your decision to transfer have on you as a parent socially?*

M: *It really didn't change. The only thing, it was just more of a conversation I had. Everyone was asking, why would you do that, why...and, once again, I wanted to give my kids a fighting chance.*

HF: *What impact did your decision to transfer have on your school-aged children socially? So, interaction with friends, uh, etc.?*

M: *Well, when they were in the district, they really didn't have that many friends, but once they transferred, it's like they just blossomed. They didn't want to come home on weekends, they wanted to stay after school more. So, I say the transfer program helped them out tremendously in that aspect.*

HF: *What impact did your decision to transfer have on you as a parent emotionally?*

M: *It... didn't really have an impact. The only..., like I just said, it was just basically I wanted my kids to have a fighting chance.*

HF: *What impact did your decision have on your school-aged children emotionally?*

M: *Emotionally, at the beginning, they were scared. Once it was final that they got their classes and their schedule, knowing their teachers, of course first-day jitters. But after a little while, they were like, "mom, it's nothing, it's just like a regular day."*

HF: *What impact did your decision to transfer have on your school-aged children academically?*

M: *I think it...it helped. They, um, they went from having homework for like, 5 minutes a day, to having it for like hours. And it didn't really bother them because they wanted to learn. They just, they just adapted to it.*

HF: *How were they academically, um in Riverview Gardens, with regards to being challenged in class. Do you see a difference between the Riverview Gardens schools and, um, and the school that your children transferred to, academically?*

M: *Um, with my middle son, he, like I said, when he was in Riverview, he was doing one grade up so that helped him transfer easier, I'm*

55

sorry, easily to the curriculum that Kirkwood had. And I think that if he didn't do that, it would have taken him longer to get to where he is. And, as far as my older son, he was about challenged the same. Because, like I said, he left before, before the transfer program, and where he was, he was doing a lot of homework but, going and doing the transfer program was a great thing for both of my children.

HF: *Were there any unforeseen challenges that your family experienced as a result of transferring?*

M: *No.*

HF: *Was there anything, um, that happened once they transferred that you didn't see happening? Either from Riverview or while they were in Kirkwood that you just didn't know that was going to occur?*

M: *No.*

HF: *As you reflect on your initial decision to transfer, as well as everything you have discussed so far today, would you change any of your previous decisions related to the Student Transfer Program? If so, why? If no, why?*

M: *I wouldn't change a thing. Because, like I said, it went from my kids not necessarily being a wallflower, but being quiet and withdrew a little bit, they just blossomed and the education that I saw that they got was also fantastic. The teachers were great. They would call, they*

56

would email. They would send anyth[ing]...they would, they would let me know how the kids were doing, they, I just, I just loved it. I just loved how the transition and the whole aspect was.

HF: *What are your views on Riverview Gardens regaining provisional accreditation on January 4, 2017, thus ending the Student Transfer Program in its current form?*

M: Well, I'm glad that it happened for Riverview. It, it's a, it's a phenomenal thing that Riverview got their accreditation back...I forgot the rest of the question.

HF: *I'll repeat it: What are your views on Riverview Gardens regaining provisional accreditation on January the 4th, 2017, basically ending the Student Transfer Law, in its curr[rent]...I'm sorry, Student Transfer Program in its current form?*

M: Um, well, like I said, I'm glad and I'm proud that it has and, you know, it's like, it doesn't affect either of my children now, because they go to the district, but if they were still in the [Student] transfer program I would bring them back.

HF: *As I extend on [that] question, basically given the education that they received the last few years, any concerns, or anything you would be, you know, thinking about as they transition[ed] back into Riverview?*

57

M: *I, it would be that...you know, it just basically like the education. It's like, just because the kids, just because the district got accredited, or provisionally, is it still you know, what would it mean for my middle aged, my middle school, my middle child when he graduates? Would that mean that his [high school] diploma meant anything? You know, that would be my only thing.*

HF: *What are your school aged children's views on Riverview Gardens regaining provisional accreditation on January 4, 2017, thus ending the Student Transfer Program in its current form?*

M: *Um, they don't know about it.*

HF: *Assuming that both of your children graduated from the school that they went to, but if their younger sibling had to attend a Riverview Gardens school, what would their views be?*

M: *Their views would be, um, take the bull by the horn. Get the best education you can, I'm here for you. I can answer any questions because that's how they are. They're, they're helpful and you know.*

HF: *One of the rationales behind the implementation of the Student Transfer Program is to ensure that all students have quality access to equitable education. So again, they want all students to have access to quality*

58

and equitable education. What does that mean to you?

M: *To me that means that anyone, you know, with any kind of education. If, if they're in the, uh, let me see, Kirkwood had the SOAR program, which is their gifted program, down to their basic classes, or down to their special ed[ucation] classes, every child has a chance.*

HF: *Did you feel that same way about the schools that your students, your children were in prior?*

M: *My middle son, when he was in elementary school, I feel did. But, like, with my middle son, I don't think so. I think that the class that he was in might have just been more kids that didn't care. I don't know. But I just had to do what I had to do.*

HF: *Based on your family's experiences with the Student Transfer Program, do you believe that this program creates opportunities for all students to receive a quality education?*

M: *Yes, I do.*

HF: *Can you expand on that?*

M: *I think that every child should have a chance at an education, and I'm glad that my children were picked for it. And I just, I'm, I'm extremely grateful.*

HF: *What is your biggest takeaway from the Student Transfer Program?*

M: *My biggest takeaway from the Student Transfer Program is that I think without it, my kids wouldn't be who they are today. But I don't know. But that's, I mean, that's what I take away from it.*

HF: *Who are your kids today?*

M: *My kids are phenomenal kids. I have a freshman in college, I have a freshman in high school, and I think without the Transfer Program that they would still be a freshman in high school and a freshman in college, but I don't think that they would have the drive, the perseverance that they have, without the Transfer Program.*

HF: *Are there any questions, or anything you wanted to discuss related to the Student Transfer Program, or your kids, that I didn't get a chance to ask you, or anything like that?*

M: *Uh uh, no.*

HF: *Based on your responses, you spoke a lot about, um, your kids and all of that. Did you have any interactions with other parents who transferred out? And if so, could you just shed a little light on what they were getting out of the program?*

M: *I only had contact with one other parent, and it was basically like the same thing. She was glad that the program was available and the same thing, for her kids to get an education.*

HF: *If your children communicated with a lot of the, uh, students who were still in Riverview Gardens. You said they didn't have too many friends...*

M: *No...they, they only had a handful. And they still, they still communicate with them as friends.*

HF: *So, given what you said, if parents are watching this and they have a kid in a transition year, what would you tell them, if they're trying to make a determination on whether they should send their children back to Riverview Gardens, or stay in whatever district they are receiving. What would you say?*

M: *What I would say is, A: follow your heart, follow, talk to your kids. You know the education that they're getting where they're at. If you're not sure, talk to the school that your child would be attending. Get everything that you can [learn] about, know everything you can about that school. The education, the teachers, principal, down to anyone that would come in contact with your child. And then, make your determination that way.*

HF: *Okay. Well, again, thank you so much.*

Tiffany's Interview (Conducted in 2017)

(HF= Howard Fields/T= Tiffany)

HF: *Without using names, can you briefly talk about your school-aged children?*

T: *Briefly talk about my school aged children...Well, I had three at the time, one elementary, one middle and one high school, at the time of transfer.*

HF: *Alright. In 2013, a judge ruled that parents in unaccredited school districts were eligible to transfer to an accredited school district via the Student Transfer Law. What were your initial views regarding this ruling?*

T: *I thought it would be a great opportunity for my kids to get a better education, in an accredited school district.*

HF: *What was the type of education you thought they were receiving, at the time in Riverview?*

T: *I didn't have a problem with Riverview, it's just that I was thinking more to the future, as far as them going to college and stuff. And I have a lot of people in my family who are educators, so they, you know, listening to them, they were telling me, like, it would have been a better move as far as, like, they transcripts... So, they broke it down to me like this: say if your child went to an accredited school and an unaccredited school, if they made straight As here, and they made straight As here, and they both want to go to Harvard, [Harvard would] pick this child that went to the accredited school first. So, it made me think, send them to the better school, and they get a better education.*

HF: *What were your school-aged children's views regarding this ruling?*

T: *My elementary child, he didn't really care either way. My, my high schooler, she thought it would be a better education, until she actually did it. My middle schooler, he don't care about nothing. But, he, they both were...basically, everybody was with going to the new school, until they got there.*

HF: *To the best of your knowledge, how did your family views regarding the Student Transfer Program, compare to your views of other families in the community?*

T: *Everybody transferred. Everybody thought it would be a better, better education, a better opportunity. Everybody in the neighborhood transferred. You know, some went to Mehlville, some went to Kirkwood, but everybody just thought it would be a better opportunity.*

HF: *What led to your initial decision to transfer?*

T: *That I thought they was going to get a better education. Like, I just was really thinking towards the future as far as high school, going to college. I was like, yeah, and I wasn't just going to transfer the high schooler one, so I was just like, send everybody.*

HF: *What impact did your decision to transfer have on you as a parent socially?*

T: *It killed me. It killed me having to have them at the bus stop at 5AM, they weren't getting home 'til 6, 7 in the evening. It, it killed me working, it killed me doing everything. I couldn't do nothing socially, but, uh, during the week, get up get my kids to school. Work a part time job in between, and then be there to pick them up from the bus stop because it was, it was such an inconvenience. The bus stop was not close to the house, like, they had one major bus stop and it was not walking distance. So, you, it['s] like...and with me having 3 children in 3 different schools...I'm there from 5AM, and got to go home and get the next kid. 6AM, go home and get the next kid. 7AM. It was, it was not good. It was not good. It wore me out.*

HF: *What impact did your decision to transfer have on your school-aged children socially? So, with other friends they had or...*

T: *It...my, my elementary schooler, he was a football player and he had to quit football behind it because he was getting home too late, getting home so late, he had to do his homework, [after] his homework, it's bedtime.*

HF: *What about your middle or your high school aged children?*

T: *They were getting home too late to do anything as well. Everybody was getting home 6, 7:00 in the evening. Then, when my high*

64

schooler, her grades start[ed] slipping, she tried to stay after school, she wasn't getting home 'til 8 or 9:00 at night. And they told her at one point she couldn't stay after anymore for the extra help.

HF: *What impact did your decision to transfer have on you as a parent emotionally?*

T: *Made me exhausted, frustrated, and it...it just emotionally drained me. Like, it drained me.*

HF: *What about your children emotionally? What did it do to them?*

T: *Well, my high sc[hooler]...well, my middle and my high schooler it, it really affected them emotionally. I just spoke with her about that. It, she was like, you know, they used to say little smart things to them. Like, the kids that come from Riverview, they only, you know, "all the kids at Riverview, all they do is get pregnant, and all them got roaches in they house" These are comments the kids was making to them. The bus drivers used to be real ignorant to them. Like, it just made them...it really made my daughter like, lose her drive to go to school. As a high schooler. And, as a high schooler, that's something that, you know, those your, them your years in school. And she was really losing her drive. She really fell behind with that transfer program.*

HF: *A lot of times, we talk about academics, so this question speaks to that. What impact did* your decision to transfer have on your school-aged children academically?

T: *My elementary schooler, it didn't, he still made straight As. My middle schooler and my high schooler, their grades dropped dramatically. My middle schooler had problems as far as the long bus ride, uh...that made him tired in class. Because he had to get up so early, so he was going to sleep in class, so his grades were dropping dramatically, it made him didn't even want to go to school. But, my high schooler, just with the social atmosphere, she wasn't fitting in. Like, it was like they had something against the Riverview kids, like, they were better than them. You know, like they felt like they were more financially stable than the Riverview kids, and all that. So, they, they, you know, they treated her like she was beneath them. So, it kind of made her just stay off to herself and it really affected her grades. She didn't want to go to class, she don't want to go to school. I'm, driving all the way to Kirkwood everyday to go get her early. She was having problems with the teachers. Her grades slipped from As and Bs to Cs and Ds.*

HF: *Were there any unforeseen challenges that your family experienced as a result of the transfer? If so, what were they?*

T: *The drive was so far, we didn't know it was going to be that far. It was like 45 minutes to an hour drive to get there. They never really welcomed the Riverview families as they did the*

Kirkwood families out there. They was like the Riverview families come for this, the Kirkwood families come for this. They never made us all one whole big family as a school district. How Riverview is, we welcome everybody. They didn't do that for us. It, it just was a bad experience all the way around. Like, emotionally, it really, it really messed my kids up. Like, as far as school, they, they never want to go back out there.

HF: *As you reflect on your initial decision to transfer, as well as everything that we have discussed so far today, would you change any of your previous decisions related to the Student Transfer Program? Why or why not?*

T: *I would have never transferred them. I would have left them at Rivervew where they felt they were at home. And they had a great relationship with the teachers, the principals, all the way around. I would have left them where they felt more safe. 'Cause, it, I had bad incidents all the way around with Kirkwood.*

HF: *Was there any positive component about transferring out, um, at all?*

T: *To me, not really. Not really. Like, I don't, I didn't see the education being better. Like, I didn't feel the teachers cared more than the Riverview teachers. They didn't, they didn't welcome us. You...I don't know. At Riverview we get that, everybody know each other, everybody welcome, even if you don't know each other, they still welcome you. You the new student, come on, you know...this such and such, we never got any of that. We never got a, "Oh, here go the principal, the vice principal..." You know, none, we never got any of the welcoming.*

HF: *What led to your decision to return to Riverview Gardens School District?*

T: *The dramatic change in my children's grades. And...overall, the way, when my children came home and expressed they feelings to me that they wanted to go back to Riverview, they wanted to go back somewhere where they felt at home and more safe. So, I just really honored they request, because I felt that they were drained. My children were drained.*

HF: *What are your views on Riverview Gardens regaining provisional accreditation on January 4th, 2017, thus ending the Student Transfer Program in its current form?*

T: *I believe that Riverview getting they accreditation back is great. Like, I believe that all the staff members, they did really work hard, and the children worked hard to help maintain that and get that back. And, as far as the children who are still in the transfer program, I know that they parents is going to be upset, but...I feel like it's going to be better 'cause we all right here. Them long bus rides is not good for them children, at all.*

68

HF: *What are your children's, your school-aged children's views on Riverview Gardens regaining accreditation on January 4th?*

T: *I just spoke with my high schooler about it. She think it's great. She loves Riverview Gardens. She want to make that her home school forever.*

HF: *One of the rationales behind the implementation of the Student Transfer Program is to ensure that all students have access to a quality and equitable education. What does a quality, equitable education mean to you?*

T: *Meaning...that they are learning everything that they need to further their self in life. Being able to go on to college and be a successful person. But I don't feel the transfer program gives them that. Like, I feel that's something they was getting at Riverview, even when they didn't have the accreditation. And I feel like it's really upon the teachers. What the teachers are teaching them.*

HF: *What is your biggest takeaway as we look now, years in the rearview mirror, what is your biggest takeaway from the Student Transfer Program?*

T: *It took my children's drive away from school. It...my high schooler and my middle schooler at the time, it really made them feel like, "ah, I don't really want to do this, I don't want to do school like this." 'Cause at first, they really had ambition, like, my son he was talking about going to college and my daughter, they don't feel that way no more. It just, since the transfer program, they were like, "no, if this is what it's going to be like, going to a new school, away from home..." They, they don't want that. And it really made them lose they drive for they education.*

HF: *If you had a parent who wanted to talk to you about, they're on the fence between sending their child back to Riverview, or staying where they're having a decent time, or even a good time for that matter, over in another school district, what would you say to them?*

T: *I would first ask them why do they feel that they, why did they even put they child in the transfer program? And, I know everybody, really they reason is going to be "I feel like it's gonna be a better education because of accreditation." A lot of people don't even know what the accreditation is though. A lot of people don't. And I would tell them, like, really sit down and talk to your child about it, because, yeah, they might be having fun and games and stuff, but, that, it...it really wears your child down from them having to be up at 4 and 5 in the morning. And you doing school from 5 in the morning till 5 in the evening. What else is your child doing with they self other than school? That would be my question to them. Because, my children were involved in other activities. They played, played instruments, football, basketball, cheerleading, and all this. So, they didn't have time for none of that being in the transfer program. So, and, that...and now, you want to talk about education? That looks good on your child's transcript, them being part of extracurricular activities and things in high school. So, you gotta think about all that. And then, when my children were in the transfer program, they didn't really give them the option of doing anything after school, because then they not getting home [un]til 8 or 9:00 at night. And they have to pay for that cab fare, so it was...it wasn't...it's not fair, and I would tell them, like, stick your children with they home school where they, you know, where they with the kids in the community where they live. You know, it, it's not no difference for real. The education not no difference. And I feel like it's just on the teachers. It, whatever the teachers, if the teachers really love the children, and they going to be there, and they love they job, and they education, they gonna make it happen for the kids.*

HF: *Were there any questions that I did not ask that you wanted me to ask, or was there anything related to Student Transfer or education in general that you wanted to speak to, that I did not ask?*

T: *No, not really.*

HF: *Okay. Well, again, thank you so much.*

Processing The Case Study

Jennifer, Michelle, and Tiffany all expressed a cursory level of initial understanding of the Student Transfer Law, which led to implementation of the Student Transfer Program. Michelle stated she was "confused about it," while Tiffany stated that her family members heavily influenced her initial understanding of the Student Transfer Law.

> *I have a lot of people in my family who are educators, so they, you know, listening to them, they were telling me, like, it would have been a better move as far as, like, they transcripts. So, they broke it down to me like this: say if your child went to an accredited school and an unaccredited school, if they made straight As here, and they made straight As here, and they both want to go to Harvard, [Harvard would] pick this child that went to the accredited school first. So, it made me think, send them to the better school, and they get a better education.*

Jennifer, Michelle, and Tiffany stated that their school-aged children's initial understanding of the Student Transfer Law primarily rested on conversations with family and friends. The common theme was that their children did not know an extensive amount about what all of this meant, other than they wanted a better education. Jennifer, Michelle, and Tiffany provided a different response when asked how their family's initial perspective of the Student Transfer Program compared with other families' perspectives within their community. Jennifer differed from many community perspectives.

> *[T]hose are the same families that got the district to where they were. Those families should have been made to remain and help get the district back to where it needed to be. The district didn't lose their accreditation because of some outside person. These people were here. When the accreditation was lost, they should have come together: town hall meetings or whatever, however, to work out a game plan, to assist the district in getting back its accreditation.*

Michelle revealed that there were mixed feelings.

> *Some families were like, "why would you leave the district, you've had them there since kindergarten." And some were like, just like with me, education. Education comes first, and that's not saying that Riverview wouldn't have had that education, but I didn't know.*

Tiffany stated that the communities' perspective was aligned with her family's perspective.

> *Everybody transferred. Everybody thought it would be a better, better education, a better opportunity. Everybody in the neighborhood transferred. You know, some went to Mehlville, some went to Kirkwood, but everybody just thought it would be a better opportunity.*

73

Social Impact

Jennifer was new to the Riverview Gardens School District during the first year of the Student Transfer Program. She described the social impact of this program on her as "challenging."

> *Well, because I'm new to the district, as a new parent, there were parents that were able to tell me their opinion of Riverview Gardens School District. And, of course, teeth and tongue fall out, so I was able to be that Well, did you try this? Did you do that? Well, naw, I did such and such and such and such. Well, you know, you can't always bail out. Because if you don't want to find out what the problem is, you just want to run, that doesn't teach your child anything. And so, for us, it was really challenging because we were bringing our children into the district, while some of our family and friends was taking their children out of the district.*

Michelle stated that her social life "really didn't change," while Tiffany could not have provided a more contrasting perspective to Michelle.

> *It killed me. It killed me having to have them at the bus stop at 5AM, they weren't getting home 'til 6, 7 in the evening. It, it killed me working, it killed me doing everything. I couldn't do nothing socially, but, uh, during the week, get up get my kids to school. Work a part time job in between, and then be there to pick them up from the bus stop because it was, it was such an*

> *inconvenience. The bus stop was not close to the house, like, they had one major bus stop and it was not walking distance. So, you, it like...and with me having 3 children in 3 different schools...I'm there from 5AM, and got to go home and get the next kid. 6AM, go home and get the next kid. 7AM. It was, it was not good. It was not good. It wore me out.*

When asked the social impact the Student Transfer Program had on her children, Jennifer did not notice an impact, stating that her children "did not miss a beat." Michelle provided a different narrative.

> *When they were in the district, they really didn't have that many friends, but once they transferred, it's like they just blossomed. They didn't want to come home on weekends, they wanted to stay after school more. So, I say the transfer program helped them out tremendously in [the social] aspect.*

Tiffany also saw a change in her children socially, as a result of the Student Transfer Program.

> *My elementary schooler, he was a football player and he had to quit football behind it because he was getting home too late, getting home so late, he had to do his homework, [after] his homework, it's bedtime. [My middle and high schooler] were getting home too late to do anything as well. Everybody was getting*

home 6, 7:00 in the evening. Then, when my high schooler, her grades start slipping, she tried to stay after school, she wasn't getting home 'til 8 or 9:00 at night. And they told her at one point she couldn't stay after anymore for the extra help.

Emotional Impact

Jennifer and Michelle stated that the Student Transfer Program did not impact them emotionally. Tiffany stated that the program "made me exhausted, frustrated, and emotionally drained me." Jennifer stated that the Student Transfer Program did not impact her children emotionally. Michelle and Tiffany felt like the Student Transfer Program did impact their children.

Michelle provided the following explanation:

Emotionally, at the beginning, they were scared. Once it was final that they got their classes and their schedule, knowing their teachers, of course first-day jitters. But after a little while, they were like, "mom, it's nothing, it's just like a regular day."

Tiffany spoke about her high schooler experiencing an emotional change because of the Student Transfer Program.

[S]he was like, you know, they used to say little smart things to them. Like, the kids that come from Riverview, they only, you know, "all the

76

> kids at Riverview, all they do is get pregnant, and all them got roaches in they house" These are comments the kids was making to them. The bus drivers used to be real ignorant to them. Like, it just made them...it really made my daughter like, lose her drive to go to school. As a high schooler. And, as a high schooler, that's something that, you know, those you, them your years in school. And she was really losing her drive. She really fell behind with that transfer program.

Academic Impact

Jennifer, Michelle, and Tiffany were all asked to consider the academic impact of their decision to or not to transfer. They all expressed that the Student Transfer Program impacted their children academically. Jennifer stated:

> [T]wo of my sons, they actually did better once they transferred into the [Riverview Gardens] school district. My other son, he was already, you know, just, he doesn't like school. So, he just did what he had to do to get by. But, two of them really excelled a great deal. Their grades, their behaviors, um, willingness to learn, studying more, reading more. They just did a lot better once they got in the district.

Michelle contributed her children's increased and continued academic performance to the Student Transfer Program.

> *I think it, it...it helped. They, um, they went from having homework for like, 5 minutes a day, to having it for like hours. And it didn't really bother them, because they wanted to learn. They just, they just adapted to it. Um, with my middle son, he, like I said, when he was in Riverview he was doing one grade up so that helped him transfer easier, I'm sorry, easily to the curriculum that Kirkwood had. And I think that if he didn't do that, it would have taken him longer to get to where he is. And, as far as my older son, he was about challenged the same. Because, like I said, he left before, before the transfer program, and where he was, he was doing a lot of homework but, going and doing the transfer program was a great thing for both of my children.*

Tiffany contributed her middle and high schoolers' decreased academic performance to the Student Transfer Program.

> *Well, my elementary schooler, he still made straight As. My middle schooler, he had problems as far as the long bus ride, uh...that made him tired in class. Because he had to get up so early, so he was going to sleep in class, so his grades were dropping dramatically, it made him didn't even want to go to school. But, my*

high schooler, just with the social atmosphere, she wasn't fitting in. Like, it was like they had something against the Riverview kids, like, they were better than them. You know, like they felt like they were more financially stable than the Riverview kids, and all that. So, they, they, you know, they treated her like she was beneath them. So, it kind of made her just stay off to herself and it really affected her grades. She didn't want to go to class, she don't want to go to school. I'm driving all the way to Kirkwood every day to go get her early. She was having problems with the teachers. Her grades slipped from As and Bs to Cs and Ds.

Unforeseen Challenges

The only participant that reported any unforeseen challenges their family experienced because of the Student Transfer Program was Tiffany. A few of the unforeseen challenges centered around transportation and not feeling welcomed.

The drive was so far, we didn't know it was going to be that far. It was like 45 minutes to an hour drive to get there. They never really welcomed the Riverview families as they did the Kirkwood families out there. They, they it was like the Riverview families come for this, the Kirkwood families come for this. They never made us all one whole big family as a school district. How Riverview is, we welcome everybody. They didn't do that for us. It, it just.

79

It just was a bad experience all the way around. Like, emotionally, it really, it really messed my kids up. Like, as far as school, they, they never want to go back out there.

Views on the "End" of the Student Transfer Program

Jennifer, Michelle, and Tiffany all responded to the question pertaining to their thoughts on Riverview Gardens regaining Provisional Accreditation, thus ending the Student Transfer Program in its current form. This rendered different perspectives. Jennifer addressed this question with both optimism and concern.

> *I think if the children are going to come back. It shouldn't be that they can come back and then start issues or problems. Or the parents and families shouldn't be able to come in and then tear up what you all here have worked so hard to get. If that makes sense. Because the teachers have worked really hard. Dr. Spurgeon has worked extremely hard. So, to get your team together to build this far, which I think it should have been more than just provisional [accreditation], but to allow those families back. I just think it should be not just, you can just walk back in the door. It's great that we, that the district has it back, but then if you bring children back in the district, who are not going to school on a day-to-day basis where they are, having behavior issues in the district that they*

are currently attending, or they're not coming to school on a day-to-day basis, then that's going to come and fall right back into the Riverview Gardens School District and put us right back where you started. So, I, I think it, it's just I don't really know how to say it, but it's kind of a catch-22 I guess.

Michelle was happy for Riverview yet appeared to have some questions.

Well, I'm glad that it happened for Riverview. It, it's a, it's a phenomenal thing that Riverview got their accreditation back. [I]t's like, it doesn't affect either of my children now, because they go to the district, but if they were still in the [Student] transfer program I would bring them back. I, it would be that...you know, it just basically like the education. It's like, just because the kids, just because the district got accredited, or provisionally, is it still you know, what would it mean for my middle aged, my middle school, my middle child when he graduates? Would that mean that his [high school] ...diploma meant anything? You know, that would be my only thing.

Tiffany appeared to be happy for Riverview Gardens as well but acknowledged that everyone may not share her sentiment.

81

> *I believe that Riverview getting they accreditation back is great. Like, I believe that all the staff members, they did really work hard, and the children worked hard to help maintain that and get that back. And, as far as the children who are still in the transfer program, I know that they parents is going to be upset, but...I feel like it's going to be better cause we all right here. Them long bus rides is not good for them children, at all.*

When asked how their children felt about Riverview Gardens regaining Provisional Accreditation, thus ending the Student Transfer Program in its current form, Jennifer had a lot to say, particularly around the role that race may have played in the decision to classify Riverview Gardens as unaccredited.

> *Well, my 7th grade son, because he doesn't really understand the whole gamut, he wants to know why did it take so long, and why only provisional. Um, so I've explained it to him as best that I can and um, and I've taken him to a couple meetings with me. I've had him look online, kind of reading some things. But it is still a lot for a 13-year-old to process, so he's still trying to understand it. Um, the other two feels like, um, can't say their terms, but they feel like the state want to play games with us because we are predominately African American school. That's the best way I can say it. Considering they're older and they clearly know what has happened. [I]f you do the research in any of the*

9 elementary schools Riverview Gardens have, the one high school, the two middle schools. So, if you check the demographics, it's predominately all minority, African American students. You can count the number of any other nationality of children that attend the district. So, in my children's eyes, and they coming from a private school, where they were 3 in the entire school. They were 3 of the 50 children that made up the school of 585 children when they were closing the building. So, they have family in various school districts, so they know, like I said, the two older ones, know, they understand and they see more, and they can have a conversation with me about when you're a predominately black school, when you're a predominately white school, what's the difference, you know. And they just feel, and that was their opinion, their words, because I hadn't even looked at it that way, but they just feel like, momma, is it because we are a predominately black district, that they playin' yo-yo, is what my oldest son said, with the kids that are in the Riverview Gardens School District. Um, he's trying to figure out why is it Riverview Gardens outscored and out tested other districts around us, but they still have full accreditation, and Riverview Gardens doesn't have it. One of the things they've said is, they have friends that, like I said, attend districts all over, um, and for my 9th grade son, his view is kind of like one of those, old type thoughts, his thing is, you know, we already are several steps

behind everyone else, but why is it those that are already behind, they're never acknowledged, you never hear about them, they're always put in the limelight, they're the ones who you always see on the sports something with the news, or whatever, I don't look at it. But whatever the sports part is on the news. But you don't see Riverview Gardens. So, I didn't have an answer, because, like I said, I don't look at the sports part of the news, so I didn't even really know too much what he was talking about. For my oldest son, his thing is, well, momma, is it that because we're always doing things this way, or we're expected to do things this way, is that why we're always on the news, versus, um, schools that really, just like, right across the bridge, have issues and things going on, but you don't hear about it. Schools right here in their back door have a lot of things going on, but you don't hear it. You always hear Riverview Gardens. So, I had to explain it as best as I felt for them to hear it, you know, that's more for you all to go to school and do better, to show those people that just because I'm, the color of my skin, does not denominate, does not say that I'm less a person or that my district is less a district, you know, because of our skin tone.

While Michelle simply stated that her children "don't know about it," Tiffany revealed her high school daughter "think it's great" and "loves Riverview Gardens."

Quality & Equitable Education

One of the rationales behind the implementation of the Student Transfer Program was to ensure that all students have access to quality and equitable education. When asked what this meant to them, as well as if they felt the Student Transfer Program provides such an opportunity, only Michelle believed that this program achieves this intended goal.

> *Kirkwood had the SOAR program, which is their gifted program, down to their basic classes, or down to their special ed classes, every child has a chance. [While in Riverview Gardens], [m]y middle son, when he was in elementary school, I feel did [receive a quality & equitable education]. But, like, with my middle son, I don't think so. I think that the class that he was in might have just been more kids that didn't care. I don't know. But I just, I had to do what I had to do. I think that every child should have a chance at an education, and I'm glad that my children were picked for it. And I just, I'm, I'm extremely grateful.*

Jennifer did not feel like the Student Transfer Program ensures that all students have access to quality and equitable education. Jennifer also had questions regarding what quality and equitable education actually means.

> *I wonder what they mean when they say that. Because you don't see [policymakers] in anybody's classroom, walking down any halls of any school. You're not coming in to help. So, instead of tearing down, come in and see what you can do to help. Teachers have it hard. They have...principals have it hard, but if you just want to keep sitting on the back burner, and you just want to keep lighting that fire even more, instead of coming in and seeing what's going on, or how you can lend a helping hand, for me, that really shouldn't even be stated. What is a quality education? They, they keep saying that and throwing that term around, but have yet to say what that really means or what that's supposed to look like. I say no [to the question]. Because a lot of the districts, I feel like they took the kids in because it was a dollar, and it was a way for them to build up their schools and increase their finances. I don't think a lot of the districts that took our children really wanted our babies out there, they just took 'em.*

Tiffany also believes that the Student Transfer Program falls short of ensuring that all students have access to quality and equitable education.

> *I don't feel the transfer program gives them that. Like, I feel that that's something they was*

> *getting at Riverview, even when they didn't have the accreditation. And I feel like it's really upon the teachers. What the teachers are teaching them.*

Four Years Later

The end of the 2016 – 2017 school year marked the end of the most recent Missouri Student Transfer Program in its current form. Jennifer, Michelle, and Tiffany provided different responses to the question: What is your biggest takeaway from the Student Transfer Program? Jennifer's response started with a question.

> *What did we really teach our children [as a result of the Student Transfer Program]? Because the ship is sinking does that mean you just abandon the ship, or do you figure out how you can do, what you can do to get the ship back up like it's supposed to be. It didn't send a good message to me. But you can still live here, but you can't be educated here?*

Michelle believes that the Student Transfer Program helped groom her children into who they are today.

> *My biggest takeaway from the Student Transfer Program is that I think without it, my kids wouldn't be who they are today. But I don't know. But that's, I mean, that's what I take away from it. My kids are phenomenal kids. I have a freshman in college, I have a freshman in high school and I think without the Transfer*

> *Program that they would still be a freshman in high school and a freshman in college, but I don't think that they would have the drive, perseverance that they have, without the Transfer Program.*

For Tiffany, the Student Transfer Program took something away from all her children.

> *It took my children's drive away from school. It...my high schooler and my middle schooler at the time, it really made them feel like, "ah, I don't really want to do this, I don't want to do school like this." 'Cause at first, they really had ambition, like, my son he was talking about going to college and my daughter, they don't feel that way no more. It just, since the transfer program, they were like, "no, if this is what it's going to be like, going to a new school, away from home..." They, they don't want that. And it really made them lose they drive for they education.*

When asked if they would change any decision pertaining to the Student Transfer Program, both Jennifer and Michelle stated that they would not. However, Tiffany's response was filled with regret in her initial decision.

> *I would have never transferred them. I would have left them at Riverview where they felt they were at home. And they had a great relationship*

> with the teachers, the principals, all the way around. I would have left them where they felt more safe. 'Cause, it, I had bad incidents all the way around with Kirkwood. I didn't see the education being better. Like, I didn't feel the teachers cared more than the Riverview teachers. They didn't, they didn't welcome us. You...I don't know. At Riverview we get that, everybody know each other, everybody welcome, even if you don't know each other, they still welcome you. You the new student, come on, you know...this such and such, we never got any of that. We never got a, "Oh, here go the principal, the vice principal..." You know, none, we never got any of the welcoming.

At the end of the 2016 – 2017 school year, the families of 437 students were faced with a decision whether to return to the Riverview Gardens School District or stay in their current transfer district. Michelle and Tiffany had a message for those weighing their options. Michelle would tell them to

> [F]ollow your heart, follow, talk to your kids. You know the education that they're getting where they're at. If you're not sure, talk to the school that your child would be attending. Get [all the information] you can, know everything you can about that school. The education, the teachers, principal, down to anyone that would come in contact with your child. And then, make your determination that way.

Tiffany would start by asking them a question.

> *I would first ask them why do they feel that they, why did they even put they child in the transfer program? And, I know everybody, really they reason is going to be "I feel like it's gonna be a better education because of accreditation." A lot of people don't even know what accreditation is though. A lot of people don't. And I would tell them, like, really sit down and talk to your child about it, because, yeah, they might be having fun and games and stuff, but, that, it...it...it really wears your child down from them having to be up at 4 and 5 in the morning. And you doing school from 5 in the morning till 5 in the evening. What el...what else is your child doing with they self other than school? That would be my question to them. Because, my children were involved in other activities. They played, played instruments, football, basketball, cheerleading, and all this. So, they didn't have time for none of that being in the transfer program. So, and, that...and now, you want to talk about education? That looks good on your child's transcript, them being part of extra-curriculum activities and things in high school. So, you gotta think about all that. And then, when my children were in the transfer program, they didn't really give them the option of doing anything after school, because then they not getting home 'til 8 or 9:00 at night. And they have to pay for that cab fare, so it was...it wasn't...it's not fair, and I would tell them, like, stick your children with they home school where*

they, you know, where they with the kids in the community where they live. You know, it, it's not no difference for real. The education not no difference. And I feel like it's just on the teachers. It, whatever the teachers, if the teachers really love the children, and they going to be there, and they love they job, and they education, they gonna make it happen for the kids.

Case Study Summary

The three (3) unique family perspectives were captured through one-on-one interviews with the mothers of these families. Their passionate stories and experiences help us, as a society, to understand the first-hand challenges that many parents must pay as collateral in the attempt to obtain "quality" and "equitable" education for their most valued possession: their child(ren). The purpose of this case study was to understand the perceptions of the Student Transfer Program by interviewing the three families from the then-unaccredited Riverview Gardens School District, who were impacted by the Student Transfer Program. This program, just like so many before it, was the latest example of what happens when policy, education, and equitable intent collide. The interpretation and lasting impact of these programs typically do not become evident until years after the program(s) end. Most of the existing literature on these programs lacks the in-depth, family perspective necessary to draw valid conclusions on how they truly impact families. There are several studies on similar topics that were able to obtain quantitative data through Likert scales and other survey data, but seldom have these studies allowed families to genuinely and thoroughly tell their stories qualitatively. Although this case study was limited to three participants, the data extracted from each participant's unique perspective helped to answer the essential questions, starting with Jennifer.

Jennifer decided to transfer her three (3) school-aged children into the Riverview Gardens School District during the first year of the Student Transfer Program. Her children previously attended a private school. Nearly four years later, Jennifer does not have any regrets pertaining to her decision to remain in the Riverview Gardens School District. Her children did quite well. In fact, Jennifer contributes her children's success to the Riverview Gardens School District. I did find it interesting that when Jennifer interacted with community members who expressed different views than her own, she took on an approach along the lines of "what are you doing to make the situation better, not worse." In addition, Jennifer also appeared to paint a picture that her family was willing to "weather the storm" and stay in Riverview Gardens to try to make things better. She felt that this would teach her children to stand up and fight for themselves. Jennifer was happy and proud of the progress that Riverview Gardens has made but was skeptical of the students who may return after transferring out to other school districts. Jennifer stated that her biggest concern was not knowing how the returning students would impact what Riverview Gardens built over the years to regain provisional accreditation.

Many of Jennifer's views could be described as "polar opposite" of the views captured by Michelle. Michelle decided to transfer her two (2) school- aged children via the Student Transfer Program, due to her concerns with one of the schools that her oldest child previously attended. While in the Student Transfer Program, her children "blossomed." Nearly four years later, Michelle did not have any regrets pertaining to her decision to transfer out of the Riverview Gardens School District. Michelle credits her children's success to the educational opportunities that were afforded by the Student Transfer Program. Michelle acknowledged that although her children excelled academically in the Kirkwood School District, she believes that the district provided all students with a chance at success. From the gifted students to the basic students, to the students requiring special education services, "all students [have] a chance." This notion was not echoed by the third transfer family in this case study.

Plain and simply stated by Tiffany, "emotionally, [the Student Transfer Program] really messed my kids up." Like Michelle, Tiffany transferred her children from Riverview Gardens via the Student Transfer Program. She stated that she wanted the best education for her three (3) school-aged children. Although Michelle and Tiffany's children attended the same district, both of their oldest children transferred to the same school. Nevertheless, their reported experiences contrasted with one another. The long bus rides impacted Tiffany socially and emotionally. She reported that two of her children were socially, emotionally, and academically impacted in a negative way, based on their experiences while in the Student Transfer Program. Tired and frustrated, Tiffany decided to transfer her children back to Riverview Gardens five (5) months into the program. Nearly four years later, Tiffany regretted her initial decision to transfer out of the Riverview Gardens School District. Tiffany also cautions other families to "stick your children with [the] home school where they live."

Altogether, Jennifer, Michelle, and Tiffany all provided information that helped to answer the two essential questions for this case study:

1. How does the Student Transfer Program impact families in the Riverview Gardens School District?

2. What experiences did families in the Riverview Gardens School District have as a result of the Student Transfer Program?

The approximately seventeen (17) interview questions for each interview participant took less than sixty (60) minutes. After reviewing all the interview data, it became apparent that there would not be a consensus found in this case study. Most of the interview responses were as different from one another as the interview participants' unique perspectives. As a result, the data suggests that the Student Transfer Program impacted families in the Riverview Gardens School District in a variety of ways. In addition, the Student Transfer Program also provided a wide range of experiences to families in the Riverview Gardens School District.

Case Study Conclusion

The original goal of this case study was to allow families with different perspectives to share their personal experiences related to the Student Transfer Program. Captured through one-on-one interviews, the extracted data were used to determine the impact of the Student Transfer Program. Such data suggests that the Student Transfer Program impacted families in the Riverview Gardens School District in a variety of ways, both positively and negatively. In addition, the Student Transfer Program also provided a wide range of experiences to families in the Riverview Gardens School District; again, both positively and negatively.

On the positive end, all the referenced students in this case study, according to their mothers, appeared to have received a "quality" educational experience. Some received such education in Riverview Gardens, some outside of Riverview Gardens. Another positive was centered on observing these mothers passionately fight for their children's education. Regardless of if you agree or disagree with the steps that were taken, one cannot argue with a parent demanding what is best for their children.

Unfortunately, there were several reported adverse effects of the Student Transfer Program. Tiffany stated that the Student Transfer Program took her children's drive away from school. This was one of my biggest takeaways from the interviews. In the quest to give students what they deserve to be successful in life, I did not think that something so precious as one's drive, could be taken because of participation in a program that was being sold as the vehicle to a better education.

In addition, it was an interesting revelation by Jennifer when she explained that her children viewed the Student Transfer Program through a Critical Race Theory lens, without ever taking a class on this subject. This appeared to have been the result of their own lived experiences. Jennifer stated that her two oldest sons felt like "the state want[ed] to play games with [Riverview Gardens] because we are predominately African American." When you examine other transfer programs such as the Voluntary Inter-district Transfer Program and the transfer programs in Charlotte-Mecklenburg and Indianapolis, to not acknowledge the role that race and poverty played in all these incidents would be fallacious, at best. Black students from "low-performing schools and districts were bused miles away from their community to attend predominantly White schools." If hours of commuting to and from school is the price for "quality" and "equitable" education, what makes the "White" schools "quality" for black students? Better yet, what makes many of the community schools that are comprised of mostly Black students "low performing?" In the St. Louis, Missouri metropolitan area, you can look at zip codes to determine the crime rate, unemployment rate, as well as the poverty rate in each area. You can also look at the zip code of a public school to determine, as well as predict, how students are performing. This brings us back to where we started. If we take students from "low performing" schools and send them to higher performing schools, in theory, this will begin to address the underline problem. But if this case study is a microcosm to more wide-ranging sentiments, then we really are further away from seeing eye-to-eye than we originally believed.

Impact of Personal Stories

Jennifer, Michelle, and Tiffany were all able to provide detailed responses to most of the questions that were asked. Though their perspectives were unique, the case study lacked in the number of overall participants. To gather a more comprehensive review of the Student Transfer Program, many more participants who are willing to share their genuine stories and experiences related to the Student Transfer Program would be needed. This includes interviewing families that transferred to more than just the Kirkwood School District. There would also be value in speaking with students and school faculty who interacted with transfer students on a regular basis. The research participants in this case study were all connected to the Riverview Gardens School District. Interviewing families from other transfer programs would have extended this research and provided more depth to the results.

All the participants had to provide, to the best of their knowledge, information regarding the thoughts and views of their school-aged children. Though powerful, some of the responses were second-hand. If students were included in this case study, the results may have been more organic.

The Documentary

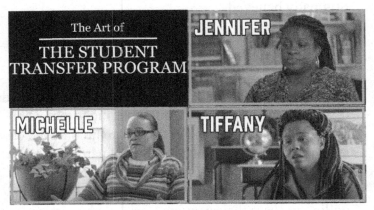

This case study was also captured in a feature-length documentary. To watch, *The Art of The Student Transfer Program*, scan the QR code below.

PART II

From A Communications Perspective

SAGE Publishing defines a crisis as a unique moment in the history of the organization. There's little doubt the districts that were either sending or receiving transfer students in 2013 were dealing with a crisis. Typically, a district communication professional communicates information on behalf of the district. For two former district communication professionals, the topic of student transfers still elicits a visceral effect ten years later. Primarily because they have never shared their personal perspectives and experiences related to this topic in a publication, until now.

Melanie Powell Robinson was the Executive Director of Communications in the Riverview Gardens School District in 2013 and Neosha Bowles was the Communication Technology Specialist in the Francis Howell School District in 2013.

These are their stories.

Melanie Powell Robinson
Former Riverview Gardens School District Executive Director of Communications

"Don't you want better?" she asked. "Don't you want better for your children? Better than what this district has given you?"

I stood across the street from the high school entrance while a young woman stood just outside the district property line to confront talk to families as they turned into the parking lot. She distributed literature to any car that slowed and attempted to engage in conversation with any cracked window. I watched her watch me. The uncomfortable exchange of non-verbal communication would not be our first, nor our last. She wanted students. She assumed that we were on opposite sides. And while we were physically standing across the street from one another, her words about wanting better, spoke to me.

It had been less than a year since I was re-hired at Riverview Gardens School District. A few years earlier, I resigned from my position as the district's Community Services Coordinator shortly before the district would undergo restructuring, be placed under state control, and receive the designation of unaccredited.

Years later, I was asked to return as the Director of Communications in my mighty department of one. The entire district's public relations and communication strategies lay right in my hands during what turned out to be one of the most followed educational stories of the region.

It was clear that my role would be to elevate and communicate to the public the district's views, while also advocating for a community that had experienced economic disenfranchisement, white flight, and an increasing number of families who did not have a long history of Ram's Pride. My role might have been clearly predefined, but my understanding of what was at stake was much more complicated.

Better. Better! Better?

Until the Student Transfer Ruling took effect and Missouri State Statute 167.131 was branded into my daily life, I had never seen this woman. She was young, blonde, and passionate. She, however, was not at any of the community meetings that I attended or hosted. I had not seen her at any of the district's board meetings or the school's open houses. I did not recognize her as a parent or district non-profit partner. I don't remember ever having seen or heard of her being affiliated with the district. But now, in this community, in my community, with my families, she seemed to know what was better.

As an African American woman, I had many conflicting thoughts about what success looks like with Black, Brown, and marginalized groups. In education, my stance was seldom concrete beyond recognizing that there was rarely an exclusively altruistic reason for people in power having concern for students of color. I was skeptical. I was optimistic. I was torn.

For years, Riverview Gardens had struggled with exceeding the academic standards that it set for itself and what was required by DESE for full accreditation. The district had endured scandals, staff turnover, financial mismanagement, and consistent negative associations. The state statute in question gave families who lived within the district boundaries– whether they had ever gone to an RGSD school or not– the option to transfer to a public school of their choice in the region. With them would be transferred more than money: but also, hope.

I reflected on "better." Of course, I wanted the best for the children in the district. I wanted them to have all of the opportunities that life could give them. I wanted them to have everything that systems robbed the generations before them. I did not want better. I wanted the best.

I knew that many of the surrounding schools had more students scoring in the "proficient," and "advanced," ranges on standardized tests. They were, indeed, many things and had many things. In most cases, they were more resourced and wealthi-er, located in areas that were farth-er, had student-teacher ratios that were small-er, and whether we wanted to say it or not, whit-er. I was unsure if they were better.

But, in contrast to "better" was "failing."

I remember feeling a strong physical response each time I heard that word or saw it in print. Having worked professionally in communications for years, I know how much words matter. I knew how certain words had been co-opted to have an underlying meaning that was applied to certain situations, in certain circumstances. "Failing" was one of those words. On its face, it did not seem to have any racial or socio-economic connotations, but, like "thug," and "gang,", "failing," became synonymous with a particular group. And it was clear to many of us just who those failures were.

Failing seemed only to be used for our students and our community. Sometimes failing was aimed at our teachers, never mind the expectation to do more with less and constant negative association with an unaccredited district. I heard community leaders, parents, and politicians lay blame at their feet.

"They must not be doing their jobs."

"They must be the teachers that couldn't get a job in a better district."

"The teachers are failing the students."

Sometimes failing was aimed at our scholars. (Yes, we chose to refer to our students as such, as many in the region seemed to use every other word but that one). There were constant reports of our students having failed state standardized tests, despite there never being pass or fail designation. How much longer would it be before the connection would be made that failing on tests would lead to failing at life?

Our district was called a failing one. We failed to move African American students whose family incomes qualified them for free or reduced lunch, to proficient or advanced categories on standardized tests. I do not ever remember seeing "failing," applied to districts with a subcategory of children, similar to ours, who consistently underperformed, compared to their regional counterparts and classmates.

I didn't think characterizing our district as having failed in many areas was incorrect. I just know that it was incomplete.

The truth was systems had been failing students in our region for years. The appetite for having these conversations only slightly elevated in 2013. Few articles and news segments took the time to report on the vast number of failures that happened upstream, long before students were not scoring as proficient or advanced on those same standardized tests. Few cameras reported on the failures long before the district was unaccredited, long before large businesses left parts of North (St. Louis) County in droves, long before segregation and unequally resourced schools created opportunity gaps, long before communities maintained wealth disparities in public education via local taxes, long, long, long ago when racism imbalanced systems. And yet, the region could not get enough of the content that the media provided. It was the educational story of the year, and no newsroom failed to report on it.

And, while not the norm, not all coverage of the student transfer system, unaccredited schools, and communities who were heavily impacted (directly or indirectly) missed the mark. There were stories, articles, and the occasional news segment that went further than the surface. Some reporters pitched story topics to editors that would give more perspectives, history, and a look at systems: but they were rare.

It is unavoidable that our biases, experiences, and perspectives creep into even the spaces that we most desire to remain neutral. Communications and media relations fields are no exception. Reporters, editors, and newsrooms with mostly white decision-makers may unintentionally frame segments or articles from a perspective that matches their own experiences and philosophies. Prominent commonly held beliefs about communities of color showed up in the reporting. Deficit thinking led to deficit narratives. Deficit narratives led to deficit language. Deficit language led to deficit actions. Day after day, I saw it, felt it, experienced it. More times than I would like to admit, I felt powerless.

Conversations around racist systems or political agendas were not normally front page above the fold or the introduction to the six o'clock news. There was a missed opportunity to lift the voices of those whose perspectives had not truly been heard in years: not heard by politicians, district leaders, board members, businesses, well-intentioned non-profit organizations, or neighboring communities. While I regret only a few things in my life, to this day I wonder if I did enough, fought hard enough, pushed back enough, screamed loud enough. I consistently advocated for a change in the pervasive narrative presented of Black students, parents, and North County communities at the center of the story. The negative framing was deafening, and I felt mute.

Parents who made decisions to select different educational opportunities for their children were pitted against those who decided to remain enrolled in unaccredited districts. Headlines, photos, and quotes highlighted differences as opposed to the similarities in the goals.

Every parent I ever spoke with wanted to make a great decision for their child. They all wanted to give their children the best opportunities to thrive and succeed even when the path to achieve this differed dramatically. They were neighbors, friends, and at times, Riverview Gardens alumni themselves. They were united in wanting the absolute best outcomes for their children, but the framing of their decisions varied greatly. Parents who wanted to send their children to schools close to home were hailed as community advocates who chose to fight to improve opportunities in their neighborhoods. Parents who wanted their children to experience the small[er] class sizes, expanded course offerings, and academic rigor that well-resourced districts were lauded to provide, were applauded as visionary and smart. As much media coverage as there was over what seemed to be an eternity, my heart ached at the notion that, once again, Black, Brown and "Broke" folks were the center of someone else's pity, mercy, and entertainment. There were lives at stake.

Meanwhile, those with true media power continued to use the current situation to report on the news, not create or reinforce narratives…right?

"Don't you want better?" she asked the vehicle in front of me.

I worried, excessively, about the experiences of the students who chose to seek different academic opportunities and transferred from Riverview Gardens and our neighboring school district, Normandy. Were they in environments where their uniqueness was valued? Were their gifts being acknowledged or were they underestimated because they came from those school districts? Were they physically tired and emotionally drained from traveling outside of their neighborhoods? Were they fairing any differently on in-class assignments and state exams? Were they making friends? Were their souls being fed? Were they- better?

Neosha Bowles
Former Francis Howell School District Communication Technology Specialist

"Do you want those kids to come to our schools?" The question I remember being asked by an elderly white male who was waving his pointer finger in my face at the Francis Howell School District (FHSD) student transfer community town hall meeting held at one of the Francis Howell local high schools.

I remember standing there, wanting to escape this entire event and conversation, but I could not. I was an employee of the district and worked in the communications department...and this event, as much as I did not want to be there, came with the job.

But I had prepared for this moment, well I thought I did.

I was exhausted, worn out, and felt defeated...And I just could not find the words. Weeks leading up to the town hall I was inundated with media calls, upset parent calls, a frenzy of social media messages and emails, and a lack of sleep. But there I was...a Black woman...allowing this man to disrespect me because he was upset, and I did not have the energy. However, I stood there with my name badge showing, holding my clipboard, preparing to address this discontented individual...but I just could not find the words...and I let this gentleman continue to scold me about his discontentment for 'those' Black kids coming to our schools.

As soon as I could flee the scene, I rushed into the girl's restroom to gather myself because tears began to flood my eyes before I could lock myself into a stall. And in that stall, I cried for what felt like an eternity, and gave myself a pep talk...I remember distinctly repeating "Neosha, get it together!"

I knew what that man meant by 'those' kids...because it was ultimately the racist remarks and stereotypes of black kids from the Normandy School District that I had been reading and hearing for months – 'those violent black kids from inner city schools who would bring our schools down; those kids who would bring guns to schools so there needed to be metal detectors installed in every school; the drug dealers who will bring drugs."

In the months leading up to the community town hall, I collaborated with school administrative officials to develop a communications plan, wrote talking points, rehearsed those talking points, took angry phone calls, and responded to hateful comments and conversations on social media and via email. But nothing prepared me more than physically being there in that moment, amongst hundreds of local community members, parents, and families who gathered to share their concerns about 'those' students who were slated to attend FHSD schools in the fall.

The Normandy and Riverview Gardens student transfer process was the start of what I did not know would be a monumental moment in my personal and professional life.

The Beginning

I was not even a year out of graduate school when I started working in the communications department at FHSD. I had interned a summer before and was lucky enough to land a full-time position. It was my first real job, real paycheck, and real-life on-the-job experience. I did not grow up too far from the District as FHSD was a rival district in my high school athletics.

I was like every student fresh out of graduate school --- ready to work and eager to start my career.

Since I had interned with the District, I was familiar with various internal processes and communications protocols, so the work came easy. However, things changed when the Supreme Court upheld the student school transfer law.

Based on school accreditation laws, Normandy School District and Riverview Gardens School District were two of the lowest performing schools in the State of Missouri and families would have the opportunity to transfer their students to an accredited school district – who was accredited and was performing at a higher level. Normandy and Riverview would be responsible for paying transportation and tuition costs for every student that would be transferring from their district. This very decision exacerbated the systemic disparities in the St. Louis region – socioeconomic status, racial divides, and fragmented geographical divides within the region.

When the decision came down, I was sitting next to the then-superintendent with no idea of what to expect. Immediately, my phone and email were consumed with media inquiries from various local outlets about this decision.

I spent the 13 weeks collaborating directly with the superintendent and District officials to communicate how we would welcome and accommodate the 400+ influx of Black students who would be bused to St. Charles County from St. Louis County to attend the predominately white Francis Howell schools.

There were several meetings that addressed concerns from administrative staff and teachers, which focused primarily on the success of all students. For example, transportation was a major concern as hundreds of transferring students would have to endure 1–2-hour bus rides to and from school. Determining the appropriate class size and student placements to ensure that classes were not overpopulated and that teachers had the appropriate tools and resources in their classrooms to help those students who may need more support. However, the number one concern that seemed to resonate across the Francis Howell parent community was school safety.

School safety is always a parent's concern for their children, and it was always a priority of FHSD. However, shortly before the Supreme Court's decision was finalized, and Normandy's selection of FHSD, local media outlets including the St. Louis Post Dispatch ran a story that placed Normandy High School as one of the most dangerous schools in St. Louis citing "assault, drugs and weapons" with 285 disciplinary incidents for the 2012 school year. This statistic and verbiage alone would terrify any parent, but this is what sent parents into an outrage of concern.

Drawing upon my knowledge from my communications studies in college, I distinctly remembered the media effects theory that explains how the media can influence the attitudes and perceptions of its audience, and this was exactly what was happening. The conversations that were happening online via social media and within the community referenced this article and others that had been reported. It was shocking and sad to read angry parents talking about their concern about Black kids bringing guns to schools, requesting metal detectors, inciting violence amongst students, selling drugs, and petitioning for the district to refuse the acceptance of incoming students.

Contrarily, there were community members and parents who were not against the decision, but those angry voices overpowered any positive comments that made it on public channels. After a while, I was not surprised when reporters started pulling comments from the District's Facebook page and incorporating them into their stories…it seemed like it was never-ending, and my days seemed to get longer and more depressing by the day.

As the days continued, there were times when I would sit in my office and just cry. This was like nothing I had ever experienced…pure direct and blatant racism. I read it daily and I did not understand how it was impacting me personally until I started to develop severe headaches. After weeks of headaches, I went to my doctor, who is also a woman of color, and explained what was happening in my life. And she told me I was under a lot of pressure and was suffering from tension headaches and anxiety. Immediately, I began to think "no I refuse to take a daily medication and I am not crazy" but the headaches began to get more intense as the days leading up to the community town hall and the first day of school was approaching...so I caved and took the medicine and to my surprised it did help but it never took away that pit in my stomach every time I took a call from an angry parent or read an email that eluded to "niggers coming to destroy our community".

When I reflect on my experience, ten years later, I internalized it all and never talked about it, because I did not want to appear as if I could not manage the job. I was fresh out of college and needed to prove to everyone around me that I could do it, but most importantly, I knew "those kids" needed me...every one of them needed me. I needed to be sure to tell their stories the best way I knew how...and I needed to somehow reframe this narrative.

A few weeks following, the Board of Education decided that it was important to hear from the parents and people in the community about this decision and they decided to host a community town hall. Being so new to the field, I did not know what to expect from this community meeting, but professional communications colleagues from the neighboring district warned me how awful this could be for the district's public relations efforts. Held at one of the high schools, hundreds of people gathered in the local gymnasium, which was filled, to share their opinions and thoughts regarding the matter.

I prepped for the meeting as best as I could...issued a press release and contacted local media outlets, sent communication District-wide, prepared handouts, wore the only professional pantsuit I owned (those came far and few being a recent college graduate), and waited for the town hall meeting to start. Groups of people, reporters, staff, and students began to trickle in, and before I knew it, the gym was full and overflow started in the auditorium.

As I was walking around, managing crowd control, that is when I was approached by the white man who I mentioned previously who decided he wanted to unload on me, one of the few Black women who worked for the district, about his discontent about Black kids transferring to the district. That moment I realized that the world was still full of racist people and that the color of my skin did matter. The local media reported on the town hall all evening – live coverage and interviewing patrons as they exited the building. I am sure if you conduct a quick Google search you would still be able to find coverage and images from the event. It is an event that I remember distinctly and quite frankly will never forget.

It was difficult for me to process because I knew that all children, regardless of race, place, and socioeconomic factors were deserving of a quality education. I was familiar with the systems that failed struggling communities and educational institutions from my own personal experience within my family. Family members fell victim to neighborhood disinvestment, single-parent homes, lack of education, and minimal job opportunities that landed them to live in areas that were considered low-income or poverty-stricken areas.

The First Day of School

The community town hall had me down for weeks, but something sparked in me, and I knew I needed to prepare for the first day of school. FHSD was the first District to start school that year and I knew that media coverage would be out of control if I did not get a handle on it first. So, after speaking with seasoned mentors, I decided that I needed to host the first day of school media day. I was completely anxious and nervous about the entire process, but I was determined to change the narrative for the transferring students. I immediately began planning...and to be honest...I did not know exactly what I was doing but I started thinking about how I could make the first day of school positive and not a scary event for the incoming families and the overall community.

I began with determining where would be the ideal location to host media for the first day of school and landed at one of the high schools that had one of the bubbliest and friendliest principals. Then I gathered students from that high school who had formed support groups to help new students get acclimated with the school. Lastly, I found parents from various schools in the district who were working with the PTOs and were also excited to welcome the transfer students. I gathered everyone together for a meeting and began to explain the importance of this day. I wanted the local media to have parents, students, and a principal to talk to about the positivity this decision brought to the district and how they were excited to welcome and support students during this transition. I did not give them talking points but wanted them to speak from their hearts and speak their truths about the importance of education. And to my surprise, everyone agreed that this was a pivotal moment for the students and families as they were making a major decision to leave their home district and enter unknown territory – unfamiliar faces, new teachers, new school, new community.

Prior to the first day of school, I developed a strategic communications plan that would inform the local press of the details of the first day of school. I arrived at 3:00 AM that morning in preparation for the first live shot for the day. That evening I could not sleep because I was so anxious.

It felt like 3:00 AM came very quickly and I headed to the high school. On the way, I was not sure what I was expecting but I was surprised at the turnout of reporters and live tv coverage that happened that morning. Every major and small media outlet showed up for this historic moment in history to cover the first day of school. The students who were interviewed shared with reporters how groups of students were serving as ambassadors to show the new transfer students around the school and that they were excited to invite them into the school. Parents shared with reporters the importance of having home support and how they were excited to collaborate with the parents of the transfer students and offer resources and support if needed. And of course, the high school principal was ecstatic for the first day of school for all students, not just transfer students, and shared how eager he was for students to begin learning.

The local journalism class even came outside to see the live coverage, and, at that moment, I asked the local reporters if they were interested in speaking with the students about their work as a journalist and why this day was a major milestone in history. The kids asked questions and appreciated the time they took to speak to them, and I was just excited that the morning was a success.

Reflections

As I think back on the entire student transfer situation, ten years ago, I did not understand the history behind the Missouri Supreme Court ruling of Breitenfeld v. School District of Clayton, which led to the then unaccredited Normandy School District to transfer students to FHSD. I ended up leaving the district the following summer because I was tired of counting the attendance numbers for Normandy students for reporters. It was clear that the media was under the impression that the students who had transferred would not withstand the long drive to and from school or that it would become too much. But to their surprise, attendance numbers remained consistent and transfer students remained in school.

Also, I wanted to alleviate myself of the stresses that came along with the entire process and decided I wanted to find a career that worked directly in putting resources back into underserved communities or helping underserved populations. But here is the thing...I really did not even know what that meant, I just knew I wanted to do more...do more for people, families and kids who looked like me. I just knew I was ready to find another job or seek an alternate career path.

Being a part of the entire process was eye-opening because I attended Fort Zumwalt School District, a neighboring school district to FHSD. During my time in school, I did not see a lot of students who looked like me, there were a few, but not a lot. I did not know at that time if any of the Black students that attended school with me lived in other areas. But one thing I did know for sure was that I was a young Black girl, and my lived experiences were and would be completely different than my white counterparts - my skin was brown, my hair was kinky-curly, which I later wanted straight to fit in with my white friends, and I talked differently.

As I got older, I also knew that anytime anyone from St. Louis asks, "what high school did you go to?" the real question is ladened with socioeconomic overtones and stereotypes that denote your level of privilege – Are you rich or poor? Did you grow up in a Black neighborhood? If you are Black, did you grow up in a white neighborhood?

My parents were fortunate enough to have the ability to choose where my brother, sister, and I would grow up and ultimately where we would attend school. But what I have come to realize is that not everyone has the option of choosing. I shared my experiences during that time with my parents, and they shared their reasons for moving to a predominately white area, and it all came down to wanting to provide for us in a way that their parents could not. My mother is from St. Louis and my father from Compton, California, and even though they grew up in different states, their families faced similar challenges - racism, lack of quality healthcare and education, the struggles they saw their parents withstand – working multiple jobs, single-parent households, living in the projects, and the lack of post-secondary education opportunities. My parents have worked hard for years to create a life that they could not be prouder of as they have watched us attend and graduate college, establish careers, buy homes, and start families.

I always said I was not sure if I could ever go back to work for the district, but ten years later, I own a home in the area and my daughter who just started kindergarten attends a FHSD school. Call it intentional or not, but I am the Black mom who cares about our kids' Black experiences in predominately white schools. There is not always a lot of us, but when there are it's important that teachers and staff acknowledge black history and not just what is written in textbooks, but acknowledge our lived experiences, our truths, and what it means to be black, especially during a time of high-profile black deaths such as George Floyd and Breonna Taylor and the Black Lives Matter movement.

I did not stick around long enough to interview any of the transfer students from Normandy, but it is my role to always advocate for Black students and be an involved Black parent in FHSD or any school district where my child resides. And I will continue to lean into being a compassionate communicator and storyteller and lean into my way of reframing the black narrative to uplift Black voices that promote equity and the excellent work of Black people and Black communities.

Race & School Rankings

The year after I completed research on the Student Transfer Program, I became an adjunct professor. I love working with future teachers and leaders for five years now! This experience gave me a rich perspective and helped me evolve as a leader. One of the most memorable learning experiences I observe from college students typically occurs during discussions on topics they are most passionate about. During a particular 2019 class discussion, a New York Times article was referenced. The article revealed that a very small percentage of Black students were admitted to New York's top eight public high schools. Soon after, a debate ignited among students on school segregation and how school rankings reinforce such segregation. About 20 minutes in, a student asked, "What are the eligibility requirements to be considered a top public high school? Another student later asked, "What are the top 8 public high schools in St. Louis County, and why are they considered the best?" The engagement these questions elicited from students piqued my interest and ultimately led to me putting my researcher hat back on and learning as much as I could about the top schools in St. Louis.

Before diving deep into this topic, it was essential to understand that using words such as "top" or "best" to describe schools is exceptionally subjective and typically leaves more questions than answers. To offset this, I examined several quantifiable measures, combined with my professional journey, to deduce a plausible answer to what school rankings reveal.

St. Louis County Finest Public High Schools

Every year, US News and World Report publishes their Best High Schools report. In this report, public high schools are ranked using the following criteria:

- College Readiness (30%) – The proportions of 12th graders who took and passed at least one AP or IB exam. Passing these exams are worth three times more than just taking the exams.

- Math and Reading Proficiency (20%) – Aggregated scores on state assessments that students may be required to pass for graduation.

- Math and Reading Performance (20%) – How aggregated scores on state assessments compared to U.S. News's expectations given the proportions of students who are Black, Hispanic and from low-income households.

- Underserved Student Performance (10%) – Scores on state assessments aggregated just among students who are Black, Hispanic and from low-income households. These scores are compared to what is typical in the state for non-undeserved students, with parity or higher being the goal.

- College Curriculum Breadth (10%) – The proportions of 12th graders who took and passed AP and IB exams in multiple areas. More exams are valued higher than fewer exams up to a maximum of four. Passing an exam is worth three times more than simply taking an exam.

- Graduation Rate (10%) – The proportion of entering 9th graders who graduated four academic years later.

According to the 2019 US News and World Report, out of the 8 Best Public High Schools in the state of Missouri, 6 were in St. Louis County.

To confirm or dispute this list, a quick search brought me to another report by Niche, an educational marking company based out of Pittsburgh, Pennsylvania. In their 2019 Best Public High Schools in Missouri report, St. Louis County was home to the 8 top schools.

The factors that are considered by Niche for their school rankings were as follows:

- Academics Grade (60%) – Based on state assessment proficiency, SAT/ACT scores, and survey responses on academics from students and parents.

- Culture & Diversity Grade (10%) – Based on racial and economic diversity and survey responses on school culture and diversity from students and parents.

- Parent/Student Surveys on Overall Experience (10%) – Niche survey responses scored on a 1-5 scale regarding the overall experience of students and parents from the school.

- Teachers Grade (10%) – Based on teacher salary, teacher absenteeism, state test results, and survey responses on teachers from students and parents.

- Clubs & Activities Grade (2.5%) – Based on expenses per student and survey responses on clubs and activities from students and parents.

- Health & Safety Grade (2.5%) – Based on chronic student absenteeism, suspensions/expulsions, and survey responses on the school environment from students and parents.

- Resources & Facilities Grade (2.5%) – Based on expenses per student, staffing, and survey responses on facilities from students and parents.

- Sports Grade (2.5%) – Based on the number of sports, participation, and survey responses on athletics and athletic facilities from students and parents.

The Best Schools by the Numbers

Ten St. Louis County public high schools were top 8 on the 2019 US News and World Report ranking or the

2019 Niche ranking. All these schools are located in affluent communities. This claim is made by reviewing these schools' assessed valuation of real estate property per pupil (AV per pupil).

The AV per pupil in Missouri in 2019 was $113,789. In the ten St. Louis County public high schools that were top 8 on either of the previously referenced lists, the average AV per pupil was $251,254, a staggering 121% more than the state's AV per pupil average. For comparison, that is also 604% more AV per pupil than some public school students also in St. Louis County.

There was also variance in poverty levels, which were determined by free and reduced lunch (FRL) populations. In 2019, 50.7% of Missouri students qualified for FRL. None of the ten St. Louis County public high schools in the top 8 rankings have an FRL population higher than 17.4%. Only two of those schools had FRL populations over 15%.

Then there is race.

In 2019, Black students comprised 35% of the St. Louis County public school population. The ten St. Louis County public high schools in the top 8 rankings all had less than 20% Black student populations. Only two of those schools had Black student populations over 15%.

So, What Do These Rankings Reveal?

I personally know many educators who worked in the ten St. Louis County public high schools included in the 2019 top 8 rankings. I can tell you firsthand how hardworking and effective these educators are.

Furthermore, as a public school advocate, recognizing local schools and their faculty for the work they do every day for students is always an accomplishment. Having stated this, when you closely examine the schools recognized as being the "best," a particular picture emerges. One that includes a small percentage of Black students and an even smaller percentage of students who qualify for free or reduced priced meals.

Moreover, the same picture persists when you review the entire list of the 2019 Best Public High Schools in Missouri. In St. Louis County, 21 public high schools had an AV per pupil more than the state average. All but one of those schools made the 2019 top 190 Best Public High Schools in Missouri ranking by US News and World Report. Of these same 21 schools, the one high school that did not make the top 190 list is the only high school with more than 35% Black student population.

In that same 2019 college course that I previously mentioned, it was stated that St. Louisans would rather read and comment on a report that was based on educational inequalities that occur in New York and not have an emotional response to it than to see the stark parallels and persistent educational inequalities that occur with great regularities in our city. My university students believed they had no choice but to see such parallels and get emotional. Many of them reported being on the receiving end of perceptions, including inadequacy for attending high schools that were "unranked" by these same entities. To quote one student, "Even though the Black and poor students in my school were outperforming some of the Black and poor children in the best schools, our school was still considered less than because of where it's located." To quote another student, "I wonder what the school rankings would be if hate speech or racist incidents within the school automatically resulted in a school being unranked."

Regardless of the entity that publishes these lists, there must be a better way of determining what makes an effective school because currently, school rankings only reveal two things: St. Louis schools remain as racially segregated as they have ever been, and when describing public schools in St. Louis, the words "top" and "best" are synonymous with affluent and a low percentage of Black students.

The Cost of The Student Program

The penalty for being unaccredited and serving over 90% Black students during the Student Transfer Program tremendously impacted the financials of the Riverview Gardens School District. Paying the tuition and transportation cost for students who transferred from their district nearly decimated their reserves. According to district documents, the Riverview Gardens School District had a 42% operating fund balance during the 2012-2013 school year, the school year before student transfers. By the 2019-2020 school year, their projected operating fund balance was 11.77%. The district saw its reserves evaporate for the second time in a fifteen-year span.

Just six years before student transfers were permitted to leave the district, a 2007 Missouri State Auditors Report revealed that the Riverview Gardens School District's financial condition had declined significantly and was expected to deteriorate further. This report revealed that the district's operating fund balance on June 30, 2005, was $12.4 million, a 20% fund balance, but was projected to be only $1.6 million, less than a 3% fund balance, by June 30, 2007. State law considered fund balances less than 3% as being "financially stressed." The superintendent during this time was later fired by the district, convicted in court, and sentenced to jail for transferring district money to his personal accounts. Court records showed he also gambled nearly $180,000 of the district's money.

Considering this context, the nearly $28,000,000, seven-year total cost of the Student Transfer Program was yet another financial blow for the then-unaccredited school district.

Fiscal Year	Tuition	Transportation	Fiscal Year Total
2013-2014	$11,055,822.08		$11,055,822.08
2014-2015	$6,427,173.35	$619,756.79	$7,046,930.14
2015-2016	$4,694,206.24	$385,158.85	$5,079,365.09
2016-2017	$3,279,947.01	$400,000.00	$3,679,947.01
2017-2018	$444,649.36		$444,649.36
2018-2019	$444,468.44		$444,468.44
2019-2020	$46,105.49		$46,105.49
Total	$26,392,371.97	$1,404,915.64	$27,797,287.61

*The Transfer Student Program began on June 11, 2013, when the Missouri Supreme Court ruled that RSMo 167.131 and 167.241 did not violate the terms of the Hancock Amendment. Student Transportation was provided by District owned buses with District employed drivers for part of the year and by First Student for the balance of the first school year (13/14). In the subsequent three school years the District contracted with First Student to provide student transportation to and from the Melville and Kirkwood school districts. The District earned provisional accreditation on January 4, 2017. Students enrolled in the Transfer Student program at that time were allowed to continue participation but no additional students were allowed to enroll in the program and the program stopped offering transportation.

New Missouri Accountability Measure

In February 2020, the Missouri State Board of Education approved the sixth cycle of the Missouri School Improvement Program (MSIP6), the newest iteration of Missouri's statewide public school accountability measure. The first APR under MSIP6 was released in 2022. Though the Riverview Gardens School District and the Normandy Schools Collaborative are two of the six provisionally accredited school districts in Missouri (as of March 2023), 112 school districts (or other LEAs) in Missouri have 2022 APR scores that are in the provisionally accredited range (50.0% to 69.9% of APR points received). Per DESE, however, MSIP6 reclassification of accreditation status is not scheduled to occur until the 2024-2025 school year. The Riverview Gardens School District and Normandy Schools Collaborative's 2022 APR scores remained in the provisionally accredited range.

DISTRICT/LEA	APR % EARNED	BLACK	HISPANIC	MULTIRACIAL	WHITE
AVILLA R-XIII	67.1%	*	7.0%	*	89.1%
BELL CITY R-II	67.2%	3.6%	3.2%	*	92.7%
BISMARCK R-V	66.2%	1.0%	4.2%	2.0%	92.7%
BOONVILLE R-I	68.1%	7.1%	2.9%	6.8%	82.1%
BRECKENRIDGE R-I	68.5%	*	*	*	96.8%
BRONAUGH R-VII	68.4%	*	*	3.8%	93.6%
CALLAO C-8	63.7%	*	*	10.6%	87.2%
CAMPBELL R-II	68.3%	*	4.7%	1.8%	92.7%
CARUTHERSVILLE	58.2%	46.4%	3.9%	8.3%	40.9%

128

18					
CENTER 58	65.0%	61.7%	11.1%	8.8%	17.1%
CHAFFEE R-II	63.4%	3.3%	1.5%	*	94.9%
CHARLESTON R-I	55.7%	62.4%	2.0%	4.6%	31.1%
CITY GARDEN MONTESSORI	68.3%	48.7%	*	2.9%	44.8%
CLARKTON C-4	66.1%	8.8%	21.4%	3.1%	66.8%
CLINTON CO. R-III	63.9%	1.9%	2.2%	11.3%	83.0%
CONFLUENCE ACADEMIES	68.1%	76.9%	15.8%	1.7%	5.2%
COOTER R-IV	67.1%	*	3.5%	*	93.0%
CROSSROADS CHARTER SCH	69.2%	43.6%	20.9%	6.3%	28.5%
DELASALLE CHARTER SCHOOL	41.1%	91.5%	5.8%	*	0.0%
DELTA C-7	64.9%	8.7%	3.5%	*	84.9%
DIAMOND R-IV	64.1%	1.0%	4.2%	3.0%	87.5%
DIXON R-I	61.8%	1.7%	4.3%	1.6%	90.8%
DREXEL R-IV	68.7%	*	3.2%	2.5%	94.4%
DUNKLIN R-V	67.9%	3.2%	4.1%	4.4%	87.0%
EAST NEWTON CO. R-VI	68.3%	0.4%	4.8%	6.1%	78.1%
EAST PRAIRIE R-II	63.0%	2.4%	1.9%	5.2%	90.3%
EL DORADO SPRINGS R-II	69.8%	*	1.4%	2.4%	95.4%
EXETER R-VI	65.5%	*	3.4%	*	85.0%
FAIR PLAY R-II	68.3%	*	1.5%	2.1%	96.0%
FAYETTE R-III	69.3%	6.5%	2.1%	5.7%	85.2%
FERGUSON-FLORISSANT R-II	66.0%	83.4%	3.8%	5.6%	6.9%

FREDERICKTOWN R-I	65.9%	0.7%	2.6%	2.2%	94.2%
GALENA R-II	63.3%	*	3.4%	3.8%	92.1%
GALLATIN R-V	68.4%	1.7%	*	*	97.0%
GENESIS SCHOOL INC.	59.2%	82.4%	4.9%	7.3%	4.9%
GIDEON 37	67.4%	*	2.2%	*	97.8%
GILLIAM C-4	59.1%	13.9%	*	*	75.0%
GOLDEN CITY R-III	69.0%	*	*	11.6%	86.0%
GORDON PARKS ELEM.	58.5%	63.5%	16.1%	11.7%	8.0%
GREENVILLE R-II	67.4%	*	3.7%	0.9%	94.8%
HAWTHORN LEADERSHIP SCH	64.0%	90.9%	*	4.1%	0.0%
HAYTI R-II	58.5%	76.9%	1.6%	*	21.5%
HAZELWOOD	65.7%	80.5%	3.1%	3.8%	11.5%
HENRY CO. R-I	68.7%	*	3.2%	1.0%	94.7%
HICKMAN MILLS C-1	62.2%	65.3%	15.5%	6.7%	9.5%
HIGH POINT R-III	67.8%	*	*	*	95.9%
HOGAN PREP ACADEMY	49.2%	89.9%	4.6%	3.7%	1.5%
HOLCOMB R-III	69.2%	*	13.9%	2.1%	83.3%
HOPE LEADERSHIP ACADEMY	68.0%	89.1%	5.0%	*	0.0%
JOPLIN SCHOOLS	69.1%	3.9%	9.9%	9.4%	71.8%
KAIROS ACADEMIES	59.2%	54.4%	4.6%	12.1%	27.4%
KENNETT 39	65.1%	31.4%	8.9%	2.4%	56.3%
KINGSVILLE R-I	69.8%	*	*	3.0%	93.9%
LA SALLE CHARTER	53.6%	98.2%	*	*	0.0%

SCHOOL					
LACLEDE CO. C-5	60.0%	*	*	*	96.9%
LIVINGSTON CO. R-III	60.7%	*	*	*	87.0%
LOCKWOOD R-I	68.3%	*	*	2.5%	94.3%
MADISON C-3	69.6%	*	3.9%	*	94.5%
MALDEN R-I	64.9%	26.1%	4.8%	5.6%	63.2%
MARSHALL	68.1%	4.6%	25.7%	5.7%	56.2%
MEADOW HEIGHTS R-II	64.8%	*	*	2.0%	97.6%
MEXICO 59	66.3%	6.2%	7.9%	9.8%	75.7%
MIAMI R-I	66.4%	*	*	5.7%	86.8%
MILLER CO. R-III	68.6%	*	*	*	99.0%
MIRABILE C-1	54.4%	*	*	*	100.0%
MOMENTUM ACADEMY	67.9%	77.1%	7.0%	6.9%	4.1%
MONITEAU CO. R-V	66.5%	*	*	*	97.3%
NELL HOLCOMB R-IV	62.4%	7.4%	*	*	90.1%
NEW MADRID CO. R-I	67.9%	27.7%	3.7%	5.8%	62.7%
NEW YORK R-IV	53.5%	*	*	*	100.0%
NEWBURG R-II	66.1%	1.8%	1.6%	2.4%	93.7%
NIANGUA R-V	66.8%	*	*	*	98.2%
NORMANDY SCH. COLLAB.	55.6%	91.4%	3.4%	3.8%	1.3%
NORTH CALLAWAY CO. R-I	62.6%	1.1%	2.2%	6.4%	89.5%
NORTH DAVIESS R-III	68.4%	*	*	*	100.0%
NORTH PEMISCOT CO. R-I	56.5%	6.4%	*	*	91.1%

NORTH SIDE COMMUNITY SCH.	66.5%	96.9%	*	1.3%	0.0%
OREARVILLE R-IV	61.4%	*	*	9.1%	84.8%
ORRICK R-XI	68.0%	*	3.1%	3.5%	92.6%
PERRY CO. 32	67.4%	0.9%	5.4%	2.0%	90.8%
PIERCE CITY R-VI	68.0%	1.2%	4.0%	*	89.9%
PLAINVIEW R-VIII	69.2%	*	*	*	100.0%
PLATO R-V	67.4%	*	1.7%	3.9%	93.3%
PLEASANT HOPE R-VI	68.4%	1.7%	*	1.0%	96.7%
RALLS CO. R-II	63.2%	1.5%	2.3%	*	95.9%
RAYTOWN C-2	65.7%	50.8%	15.0%	9.1%	23.4%
RICHMOND R-XVI	57.6%	1.9%	1.8%	6.5%	88.6%
RICHWOODS R-VII	68.1%	*	*	*	96.8%
RIDGEWAY R-V	66.9%	*	*	*	100.0%
RIPLEY CO. R-IV	61.9%	*	*	*	96.6%
RITENOUR	67.3%	42.8%	25.2%	8.2%	22.1%
RIVERVIEW GARDENS	62.4%	97.1%	1.6%	*	1.1%
SCOTT CO. CENTRAL	68.7%	17.8%	*	13.0%	68.9%
SENATH-HORNERSVILLE C-8	65.1%	*	37.4%	2.5%	59.4%
SLATER	68.8%	4.0%	4.0%	9.2%	82.5%
SOUTH PEMISCOT CO. R-V	65.6%	20.3%	4.9%	8.5%	65.9%
SOUTHWEST R-V	69.8%	*	5.0%	2.3%	89.0%
ST. JOSEPH	67.6%	6.6%	10.7%	10.3%	68.3%

ST. LOUIS CITY	63.8%	77.8%	6.7%	0.9%	12.0%
ST. LOUIS LANG IMMERSION SCH	52.4%	54.7%	18.8%	10.3%	15.1%
STEWARTSVILLE C-2	67.1%	*	*	3.3%	95.6%
STURGEON R-V	65.1%	*	*	5.5%	92.5%
SUCCESS R-VI	67.3%	*	*	*	100.0%
SUNRISE R-IX	60.0%	*	3.0%	1.7%	94.0%
THE ARCH COMMUNITY SCH.	58.3%	96.8%	*	*	0.0%
TRI-COUNTY R-VII	67.5%	*	3.2%	*	94.3%
UNIVERSITY CITY	69.2%	78.7%	5.4%	4.1%	10.9%
VAN BUREN R-I	59.6%	*	1.6%	1.6%	95.6%
VAN-FAR R-I	62.8%	3.3%	2.4%	7.4%	86.9%
VERONA R-VII	65.8%	*	34.9%	1.5%	61.2%
WARREN CO. R-III	64.2%	3.0%	5.7%	6.3%	84.4%
WARSAW R-IX	68.5%	0.7%	2.2%	3.9%	92.3%
WINFIELD R-IV	67.4%	1.0%	1.7%	4.1%	92.9%

*2022 Missouri APR results for provisionally accredited and unaccredited school districts/LEAs

Of the 45 school districts (or other LEAs) in Missouri with student populations that are majority Black, 37.8% scored in the fully accredited range (70.0% to 94.9% of APR points received), 57.8% scored in the provisionally accredited range (50.0% to 69.9% of APR points received), and 4.4% scored in the unaccredited range (less than 50.0% of APR points received).

DISTRICT/LEA	APR % EARNED	BLACK	ACCREDITATION RANGE
KIPP: ENDEAVOR ACADEMY	70.30%	73.8%	Accredited
JENNINGS	70.60%	97.5%	Accredited
LIFT FOR LIFE ACADEMY	70.60%	96.9%	Accredited
KANSAS CITY 33	70.60%	51.9%	Accredited
LEE A. TOLBERT COM. ACADEMY	71.20%	88.5%	Accredited
THE BIOME	71.20%	82.5%	Accredited
KIPP ST LOUIS PUBLIC SCHOOLS	71.30%	95.9%	Accredited
GRANDVIEW C-4	71.70%	47.0%	Accredited
KC INTERNATIONAL ACADEMY	73.50%	59.9%	Accredited
SCUOLA VITA NUOVA	73.50%	40.0%	Accredited
CITIZENS OF THE WORLD CHARTER	73.70%	38.7%	Accredited
KANSAS CITY GIRLS PREP ACADEMY	77.80%	68.2%	Accredited
ACADEMY FOR INTEGRATED ARTS	79.90%	81.3%	Accredited
UNIVERSITY ACADEMY	81.70%	94.5%	Accredited
BROOKSIDE CHARTER SCH.	82.20%	88.0%	Accredited
EWING MARION KAUFFMAN SCHOOL	83.40%	81.4%	Accredited
ATLAS PUBLIC SCHOOLS	91.60%	72.8%	Accredited
ST. LOUIS LANG IMMERSION SCH	52.40%	54.7%	Provisionally Accredited
LA SALLE CHARTER SCHOOL	53.60%	98.2%	Provisionally Accredited
NORMANDY SCHOOLS COLLABORATIVE	55.60%	91.4%	Provisionally Accredited
CHARLESTON R-I	55.70%	62.4%	Provisionally Accredited
CARUTHERSVILLE 18	58.20%	46.4%	Provisionally Accredited

THE ARCH COMMUNITY SCHOOL	58.30%	96.8%	Provisionally Accredited
HAYTI R-II	58.50%	76.9%	Provisionally Accredited
GORDON PARKS ELEM.	58.50%	63.5%	Provisionally Accredited
GENESIS SCHOOL INC.	59.20%	82.4%	Provisionally Accredited
KAIROS ACADEMIES	59.20%	54.4%	Provisionally Accredited
HICKMAN MILLS C-1	62.20%	65.3%	Provisionally Accredited
RIVERVIEW GARDENS	62.40%	97.1%	Provisionally Accredited
ST. LOUIS CITY	63.80%	77.8%	Provisionally Accredited
HAWTHORN LEADERSHIP SCHL GIRLS	64.00%	90.9%	Provisionally Accredited
CENTER 58	65.00%	61.7%	Provisionally Accredited
HAZELWOOD	65.70%	80.5%	Provisionally Accredited
RAYTOWN C-2	65.70%	50.8%	Provisionally Accredited
FERGUSON-FLORISSANT R-II	66.00%	83.4%	Provisionally Accredited
NORTH SIDE COMMUNITY SCHOOL	66.50%	96.9%	Provisionally Accredited
RITENOUR	67.30%	42.8%	Provisionally Accredited
MOMENTUM ACADEMY	67.90%	77.1%	Provisionally Accredited
HOPE LEADERSHIP ACADEMY	68.00%	89.1%	Provisionally Accredited
CONFLUENCE ACADEMIES	68.10%	76.9%	Provisionally Accredited
CITY GARDEN MONTESSORI	68.30%	48.7%	Provisionally Accredited
UNIVERSITY CITY	69.20%	78.7%	Provisionally Accredited
CROSSROADS CHARTER SCHOOLS	69.20%	43.6%	Provisionally Accredited

DELASALLE CHARTER SCHOOL	41.10%	91.5%	Unaccredited
HOGAN PREPARATORY ACADEMY	49.20%	89.9%	Unaccredited

*2022 Missouri APR results for school districts/LEAs that serve majority Black students

For districts across Missouri, their pending MSIP6 accreditation statuses will have long-lasting implications. Missouri Revised State Statute 162.085 includes language that if a school district (or other LEA) has been classified as unaccredited within the previous five years and the district (or other LEA) is subsequently classified as provisionally accredited, the district (or other LEA) shall be subject to lapse on June thirteenth of any school year in which the State Board of Education withdraws provisional accreditation or at a later date determined by the State Board of Education.

OPEN ENROLLMENT

On May 12, 2023, the Missouri legislative session adjourned without taking a vote on Missouri House Bill 253. This bill established transfer procedures to nonresident districts for students in public education. For years, similar bills have been debated by policymakers. Four years before the Student Transfer Law was upheld, the Missouri Joint Committee on Education prepared a 2009 report for the General Assembly focusing on interdistrict open enrollment in Missouri. At the time, there were six existing interdistrict open enrollment options for Missouri students via Missouri State Statutes:

- RSMo. 167.121.1 - The Commissioner of Education may assign a student to a district other than the district of residence if the attendance in the district of residence would create a transportation hardship.

- RSMo. 167.121.2 - A parent or guardian may enroll his or her child in Missouri's virtual school if the district of residence is lapsed, unaccredited, or provisionally unaccredited for two consecutive years.

- RSMo. 167.131 - The Board of Education of a district that does not maintain an accredited school must pay the tuition and transportation for students to attend an adjacent district.

- RSMo. 167.151 - The Board of Education of a district may allow nonresident students to attend school in the district without paying tuition in some circumstances.

- RSMo. 162.1045 - The State Board of Education shall direct DESE to develop guidelines for an optional open enrollment pilot program.

- RSMo. 162.1060 - "Metropolitan Schools Achieving Value in Transfer Corporation", an urban voluntary school transfer program, established.

This same report examined the 14 open enrollment states operating in 2009. In those states, participation among public school students was between 0.5% to 18.8%.

It is also important to note that race was a concern during a Missouri public hearing on open enrollment. Several individuals voiced concern that open enrollment could be divisive by race and class. Missouri House Bill 253 explicitly mentioned academic and competitive entrance exams being part of the proposed open enrollment admission process. Considering students could also be denied transfer admission based on their discipline record, subtle and obvious discriminatory practices would likely occur. Last year in the *Peabody Journal of Education*, Sampson, Garcia, Hom, & Bertrand stated that open enrollment was a "wolf in sheep's clothing" because of the eventual shutdown of underperforming schools due to under-enrollment. Additionally, they found the following six significant concerns ultimately plague open enrollment efforts:

- Students of color and students from lower-income families bear the burden. Rather than providing every student with local options that meet their needs, open enrollment shifts the burden of attaining a high-quality education to the families. Because neighborhoods that serve larger shares of low-income families and students of color tend to have lower-performing schools, these are the students who bear the burden of lengthy commutes to neighborhoods with higher shares of white and affluent families—which tend to have higher-performing schools.

- Open enrollers may encounter racism. When students of color open enroll in majority white schools, they may encounter a racist environment in which they disproportionately suffer consequences such as higher rates of exclusionary discipline and lower rates of enrollment in college preparatory classes.

- Families who participate in inter-district open enrollment send their children to schools in jurisdictions where they can't vote. As a result, although they may at times get school officials to listen to them or meet their needs, parents who are voters in the district may have more clout. Rather than merely voting against disfavored school board members, open enrolling families who do have concerns must take more time-consuming and elaborate steps to make themselves heard—such as demonstrating repeatedly at school board meetings.

- "Voting with your feet" is more complicated than it may seem. A justification of open enrollment is that families vote with their feet. However, for students of color whose local schools are of low quality or not meeting their needs, the choices may each be untenable. For instance, they can either remain in a place where they encounter high levels of racism or transfer back to local schools with fewer instructional resources.

- School ratings are flawed. Parents are often encouraged to transfer from schools with lower accountability ratings to schools with higher ratings. Yet these rating systems are themselves flawed in that they tend to focus mainly on average results of standardized tests without taking into account harder-to-measure yet equally important factors such as equity or cultural competence. As a result, lower-rated schools, no matter their overall quality, will lose enrollment and risk closure while higher-rated schools attract open enrollees (and the additional per-pupil funding that accompanies them) whom they don't serve well.

- Open enrollment creates winners and losers. Even when they have similar incomes to their neighbors whose children do not open enroll, open enrollers tend to have more resources and social capital. In order to open enroll, a parent needs to be aware that open enrollment is an option, proficient at navigating the bureaucratic requirements associated with school choice, and (in the many states where transportation is not provided to open enrollers) able to take their children to and from schools that are farther from home than their local options. The schools left behind therefore lose parents who would have had more wherewithal to demand improvements. Similarly, the children who leave tend to have more opportunities to learn and academic supports outside of school. When a school has a concentration of students with very high levels of academic need because those with lower need levels have departed, that school's accountability ratings tend to drop, and when more politically powerful parents opt out, school resources tend to drop (on top of the lost per-pupil payments when any student leaves). This feeds an ongoing cycle.

In 1988, the state of Minnesota began open enrollment. Per a 2013 study by the University of Minnesota that examined thousands of students, open enrollment increased racial segregation. Among the key findings was that White students who chose to participate in open enrollment often left diverse school districts to attend schools with a higher percentage of White students. Missouri House Bill 253 proposed restricting the number of transferring students to 3% of the previous school year's enrollment. This was viewed as a strategy to curb the potential influx of students to or from a school district (or other LEA). Even with the proposed cap, school districts (and other LEAs) would potentially still see a decrease in funding that could be deemed significant.

DISTRICT/LEA	2022 K-12 Student Enrollment	3% K-12 Student Enrollment
ACADEMY FOR INTEGRATED ARTS	241	7
ATLAS PUBLIC SCHOOLS	114	3
BROOKSIDE CHARTER SCH.	717	22
CARUTHERSVILLE 18	939	28
CENTER 58	2410	72
CHARLESTON R-I	763	23
CITIZENS OF THE WORLD CHARTER	517	16
CITY GARDEN MONTESSORI	279	8
CONFLUENCE ACADEMIES	2444	73
CROSSROADS CHARTER SCHOOLS	1072	32
DELASALLE CHARTER SCHOOL	189	6
EWING MARION KAUFFMAN SCHOOL	1089	33
FERGUSON-FLORISSANT R-II	9237	277
GENESIS SCHOOL INC.	205	6
GORDON PARKS ELEM.	137	4

GRANDVIEW C-4	3636	109
HAWTHORN LEADERSHIP SCHL GIRLS	121	4
HAYTI R-II	615	18
HAZELWOOD	16313	489
HICKMAN MILLS C-1	4810	144
HOGAN PREPARATORY ACADEMY	1008	30
HOPE LEADERSHIP ACADEMY	119	4
JENNINGS	2347	70
KAIROS ACADEMIES	412	12
KANSAS CITY 33	13270	398
KANSAS CITY GIRLS PREP ACADEMY	176	5
KC INTERNATIONAL ACADEMY	654	20
KIPP ST LOUIS PUBLIC SCHOOLS	2627	79
KIPP: ENDEAVOR ACADEMY	675	20
LA SALLE CHARTER SCHOOL	112	3
LEE A. TOLBERT COM. ACADEMY	391	12
LIFT FOR LIFE ACADEMY	797	24
MOMENTUM ACADEMY (EAGLE PREP)	837	25
NORMANDY SCHOOLS COLLABORATIVE	2764	83
NORTH SIDE COMMUNITY SCHOOL	455	14

RAYTOWN C-2	7757	233
RITENOUR	6203	186
RIVERVIEW GARDENS	5157	155
SCUOLA VITA NUOVA	380	11
ST. LOUIS CITY	17135	514
ST. LOUIS LANG IMMERSION SCH	437	13
THE ARCH COMMUNITY SCHOOL	95	3
THE BIOME	166	5
UNIVERSITY ACADEMY	1106	33
UNIVERSITY CITY	2392	72

*2022 Missouri K-12 enrollment totals & 3% of student count for school districts/LEAs that serve majority Black students

All students should have access to a quality educational experience. Too often, however, the expense of policies that attempt to achieve this goal has resulted in continuous denigration of Black school communities.

The Denigration of Black School Communities

A reenactment is the acting out or repetition of a past event. Reenactments can depict the original so accurately that those who do not have historical context could be left to think what they are witnessing is an original. Most educational policies established to help Black students in Missouri and across the country over the past 50 years have been reenactments. Not only is the entire storyline a repeat but so are the outcomes, which we have all seen several times.

Case and point: Someone recognizes that not all students have adequate resources to flourish in school. Contributing factors vary from local funding sources to systems and practices within the school itself. Frequently, primarily in metropolitan areas, the student's race is a significant indicator that perpetuates learning and opportunity gaps. This results in a desire to do something about the observed inequities. A barrier emerges after a few initial steps toward achieving educational equity- too many influential people within the school and community are not comfortable discussing race. It does not matter that the data substantiates that we are not meeting the needs of our Black students and must discuss race to address such stark disparities. Power and influence prevail over leadership and humanity, resulting in stagnation. The students who need aggressive change continue to plateau or, even worse, continue their academic descent. Meanwhile, those serving as barriers find solace in knowing that regardless of their inaction, simply reiterating their dedication to this work and the success of all students is enough to make it through their term, tenure, or election.

In a move considered a compromise to discussing race, euphemisms and other coded language are used to continue the conversation. For those most passionate and historically agitated by the lack of organizational action, they can only hope that the most recent plan will be the start of continuous and necessary work. To help garner more support from previous opposers, other student groups are identified as also needing additional support. When this occurs, a hierarchy is established within the co-opted language, reinforcing the same inequities and disparities that initiated such discussions. What is now viewed by some as a more inclusive plan shifts to being equality based, where everyone benefits. This decision widens racial gaps but does serve as a checklist and feel-good tactic.

Next, a policy, procedure, and in some cases, a law is enacted. What started as an intentional quest to support a particular group of students mutates into more general support for everyone. There is little doubt that all students benefit from layers of support. Nevertheless, when support for all comes at the expense of creating or eliminating policies, systems, and practices that impact the experiences, outcomes, and access to resources for Black students, the cycle of school being overly empathetic to the needs of Black students yet underly actionable at the same time persists. More harm is caused as time passes, and even the biggest supporters of these efforts grow in frustration. A committee is then formed to review and recommend amendments to the existing plan. More resources, including personnel, are added to the updated plan. Then the story repeats itself over and over and over again.

For the Black students and communities whose voices and best interests were never as much of a priority as it should have been, frustrations grow, and increasingly critical views of the educational landscape take hold. Considering the history of how neighborhoods across the country, including the St. Louis area, have become as they are, there are more sinister parallels between schools and communities that cannot be ignored.

Richard Rothstein's book "The Color of Law" argues that St. Louis is an example of how government policies created and reinforced racial segregation in America's cities. More specifically, Rothstein cited the following government-sanctioned segregation strategies:

- Redlining: The federal government and private lenders designated specific neighborhoods in St. Louis as "hazardous" or "risky" for mortgage lending, leading to disinvestment in those areas and making it difficult for African Americans to obtain home loans.

- Racially restrictive covenants: These were agreements between White homeowners not to sell their homes to African Americans, effectively creating racially segregated neighborhoods.

- Zoning laws: St. Louis enacted laws that prohibited apartment buildings in certain areas, making it harder for African Americans to find affordable housing in desirable neighborhoods.

- Urban renewal: St. Louis used federal funds to demolish predominantly African American neighborhoods, displacing residents and further segregating the city.

These intentional efforts created and reinforced racial segregation in St. Louis and other American cities. The relationship between schools and neighborhoods makes it necessary to understand racial segregation's impact on schools today. Though these actions have been outlawed, you will see how these same practices still exist in schools today by adjusting the language to codify school-specific context.

- Redlining (in schools): Designating specific schools in St. Louis as "the top" or "the best" and others as "hazardous" or "risky," affecting home ownership in those areas and making it difficult for predominantly African American schools to obtain adequate local funding.

- Racially restrictive covenants (in schools): The practice of redistricting school boundaries along racial lines. This practice involves drawing school attendance boundaries in a way that intentionally or unintentionally creates racially segregated schools and limits enrollment based on race.

- Zoning laws (in schools): St. Louis still has zoning laws when considering district boundary lines. School district boundaries significantly impact school demographics, resources, and academic performance. With gentrification occurring in St. Louis, it can still be difficult for African Americans to find affordable housing in well-resourced school districts.

- Urban renewal (in schools): School closures and consolidations displace students and teachers and disrupt social networks. These tactics have primarily been used to address declining enrollment, budget constraints, or racial segregation in schools that disproportionately affect low-income communities and communities of color.

Many believe that an open enrollment bill will likely pass in Missouri within the next few years. If it does pass, there is little doubt that school districts serving predominantly Black students and communities will lose a significant portion of their funding. The argument needs to be more about whether the Student Transfer Program or recent open enrollment attempts accomplishes the goals associated with school choice. The issue lies in continuously denigrating Black and already under-resourced school communities to accomplish what is being sold as increased options for students and their families. The discussion we should be having is how to fund all schools adequately.

In 2019, news about a possible St. Louis City and County merger was quite the topic of discussion. Some of the details of the proposed merger included approximately 320 additional police officers and a budget increase of 74 million dollars. Imagine how schools could benefit from 300 more educators and 70 million additional dollars to better meet the needs of students. Though a hypothetical scenario with no way of knowing if the increase in staff and funding would be commensurate to the increase in police officers and money, should we not consider this option from an educational standpoint? If a merger between St. Louis City and County school districts could increase students' educational access and opportunities, I believe we have a responsibility to explore such a thought.

According to DESE, in 2019, 162,165 public school students were enrolled in the 25 school districts in St. Louis City and County. To better understand the inequities among these districts, one must start with the funding disparities. As provided in a prior section, the assessed valuation of some districts results in rich educational experience for their students. To state that there is variance in these figures within St. Louis City and County school districts would be an understatement. The average assessed valuation per pupil in Missouri in 2019 was $113,789. In St. Louis, there were nine school districts below this mark. Additionally, there was as much as a $78,082 per pupil disparity between some students in St. Louis compared to the Missouri per pupil average. The figures are more appalling when examining the assessed valuations of districts only in St. Louis. There was as much as a $394,128 assessed valuation per pupil disparity between St. Louis students approximately 10 miles apart (Clayton and Riverview Gardens). This inequity would be nearly eliminated if St. Louis City and County school districts merged. All 162,165 students (2019 figures) would have received more than the state's average assessed valuation per pupil by $61,396 ($175,184).

As with any bold proposal to change, there will be much criticism and pushback on merging or consolidating school districts. Concerns over the number of students in this hypothetical school district would cause hysteria for some. However, school consolidation in St. Louis is familiar. If you recall, the presiding judge in the Liddell v. Board of Education case threatened to combine and consolidate multiple districts into one metropolitan school district in 1983. Forty years later, it may be time to revisit this consideration.

Moreover, if we only consider safe solutions, we run the risk of exacerbating the problems. There would be many benefits of having such a large district. A complaint we often hear in education is the cost of insurance and the relatively low pay. Many educators work an additional job to "make ends meet." A survey by the US Department of Education revealed that 19% of teachers in the Midwest work an additional job to supplement approximately $5,000 in income. This statistic is not surprising when you consider the number of educators from smaller and less-resourced districts that leave for the larger, better-paying districts. Schools that serve many minority students know this all too well. They often rely on inexperienced or non-certificated staff to fill their staff vacancies. Creating such a large district should enable more effective practices in addressing discrepancies in teacher pay and providing more affordable insurance for educators' families. Although a large school district would be new to St. Louis, large school districts are not uncommon in metropolitan areas. In 2019, there were 16 school districts in the US with enrollments over 150,000. These districts report considerable savings by cutting operational costs and providing students with more resources, namely access to advanced placement courses, increased elective and specialized course options, and more attractive grants.

In California, the Los Angeles Unified School District has 730,000 students. They have credited their large size as a determining factor in supporting students with special needs, which includes providing the personnel to help integrate students into general education classes. School district consolidation may be less widespread for schools and communities, but some legislators favor it. In 2007, a school district consolidation law was passed in Maine, reducing the state's 290 school districts to approximately 80. Out of this mandate was consolidating 92 school districts down to 24 districts. In Maryland, New Jersey, and Virginia, state legislators have passed laws prohibiting more than one school district per county. Imagine if Missouri legislators were to follow suit.

As an educational advocate, I am intrigued and cautious when I hear of proposed solutions to address complex inequities in our educational system. Past St. Louis City-County merger proposals did not include a plan to merge school districts. However, what if they did? Remaining closed-minded about any idea or possible solution could eventually lead to bigotry, which in some regard, forces us to examine if we are advocating for a cause or just our own beliefs. While consolidating or merging schools in St. Louis City and County into one or more school districts would address some of the equity and funding issues pervasive in our region, I do not view such an idea as plausible in St. Louis. Education has become a great example of opposites and extremes; you cannot have one without another. Nationally recognized "great" schools and districts need schools and districts that are perceived as "bad" to magnify their greatness, even when the data in some cases show that their Black students are performing no better or worse than the Black students in the predominantly Black schools.

The same can be said about rich and poor school districts, which have created the newest form of segregation. A similar belief was shared by EdBuild, a nonprofit that focuses on public school funding equity, regarding their report on merging school districts:

> *By allowing our public education system to be separated into territories of haves and have-nots, we reproduce our wider social inequality in the schools that should be the opposite: The ladder that enables mobility and greater equality for all. Instead, we allow segregation to develop as the wealthy sort themselves into advantaged districts, leaving the needy districts behind.*

All entities and organizations work extremely hard to protect their statuses and positions. Furthermore, although equity may be a desirable outcome for people, the overwhelming majority appear unwilling to ensure equity at the expense of their statuses and positions, including their school district. There would be some loss of local control, concerns with redrawing attendance boundary lines, impact on school diversity, teacher quality, and many other reasons why people may vehemently oppose consolidating or merging districts. While some are legitimate concerns with merging school districts, many are not. Nevertheless, as DESE Deputy Commissioner Dr. Stacey Preis alluded, finding the shortcomings in a potential solution without providing a better solution is not a solution; it just adds to the problem. For St. Louis, our persistent educational problems have resulted from our unwillingness to implement bold measures to ensure educational justice. There may be some individual student success stories that can be attributed to school integration (1954), the St. Louis Desegregation Program (1984), or the Student Transfer Program (2013), but the long-lasting impact of these efforts are still best described as reenactments of the same story, which can be accurately titled, The Denigration of Black School Communities. A story that, in another 50 years, will have updated language and a new cast, but an ending that we would have already seen.

REFERENCES

A Primer to the Outstanding Schools Act (1993). Missouri's Governor's Office. Jefferson City, MO.
Andrews, M., Squire, C. & Tamboukou, M. (2013). Doing narrative research. Los Angeles: Sage Publishing
Barbour, R. S. (2001). Checklists for improving rigor in qualitative research: A case of the tail wagging the dog. British Medical Journal, 322, 1115-1117.
Beckwith, L. (2016, December 8). Personal interview.
Beckwith, L. (2016, December 10). Personal interview.
Beckwith, L. (2017, March 22). Personal interview
Bock, J. (2012). State board gives provisional accreditation for St. Louis Public Schools. St. Louis Post Dispatch. Retrieved from: http://www.stltoday.com/news/local/education/stateboard-gives-provisionalaccreditation-for-st-louis-public-schools/article_27dc69e-596a 5c4f-a5ade5c8d224971f.html
Bollen, K. A. (1989). Structural equations with latent variables. New York: Wiley.
Bose, R. (2012). So you've lost accreditation, what now? A how-not-to guide from Kansas City and St. Louis. nextSTL. Retrieved from: https://nextstl.com/2012/04/so-youve-lostaccreditation-what-now-a-how-to-hownot-to-guide-from-kansas-city-and-st-louis/
Boustan, L.P. (2010). Was postwar suburbanization "white flight"? Evidence from the black migration. Quarterly Journal of Economics (February). 417-443. Retrieved from: http://www.econ.ucla.edu/lboustan/research_pdfs/research02_whiteflight.pdf
Breitenfeld v. School District of Clayton (2013). Supreme Court of Missouri.
Brown v. Board of Education (1954). Supreme Court of the United States.
Byrne, M. M. (2001). Evaluating findings of qualitative research. AORN Journal, 73, 703- 704. Civil Right Glossary. (n.d.). Retrieved from: http://www.civilrights.org/resources/civilrights101/glossary.html
Clandinin, D.J. & Connelly, F. M. (1990). Stories of experience and narrative inquiry. Educational Researcher, 19(5), 2-14. The Missouri Student Transfer Program 117
Cobbe, S. (1990). Education indicators for policy purposes in Indonesia. Jakarta: Ministry of Education and Culture.
Coffey, A., & Atkinson, P. (1996). Making sense of qualitative data: Complementary research strategies. Thousand Oaks, CA: Sage Publishing.
Court upholds decision to rescind St. Louis Public School's accreditation (2008). St. Louis Business Journal. Retrieved from: http://www.bizjournals.com/stlouis/stories/2008/01/21/daily43.html
Crouch, E. (2016). St. Louis desegregation program headed for phase out. St. Louis Post Dispatch. Retrieved from: http://www.stltoday.com/news/local/education/stlouisdesegregation-program-headed-for-phase-out/article_9dadfa4c-3d49-5b80-b6ec2b1c03d2e5c7.html
Davis, T.J. (2004). More than segregation, racial identity: The neglected question in Plessy v. Ferguson. Washington and Lee Journal of Civil Rights and Social Justice, 10(1). 1-43.
Domenech, D. (2011, January 28). Ohio Case: The 'Rosa Parks moment' for education [radio interview]. National Public Radio. Retrieved from:

http://www.npr.org/2011/01/28/133307552/ohio-case-the-rosa-parksmoment-foreducation

Elementary and Secondary Education Act (1965). Congress of the United States, Washington, D.C.

Ellis, C., Adams, T.E., & Bochner, A.P. (2011). Autoethnography: An overview. Forum: Qualitative Social Research, 12 (1).

Every Student Succeeds Act (2015). Executive Office of the President. Washington, D.C.

Fields, H. (2012). St. Louis desegregation program & its impact on high school sports (unpublished paper). University of Missouri, St. Louis.

Fields, H. (2021). How To Achieve Educational Equity (Dr. Howard E. Fields III, LLC).

Flentroy, G.L. (1977). The struggle of blacks for equal educational opportunity: An overview. Hastings Constitutional Law Quarterly, 4(Summer), 605-635.

Gall, M.D., Gall, J.P., & Borg, W.R. (2007). Educational research: An introduction. Pearson, New York. Glaser, D. (n.d.). Frequently asked questions. Retrieved from: http://www.choicecorp.org/FAQ.pdf

Gotham, K.F. (2002). Missed opportunities, enduring legacies: School segregation and desegregation in Kansas City, Missouri. American Studies, 43(2). Retrieved from: https://journals.ku.edu/index.php/amerstud/article/view/3050

Grace, K. (2014). De facto segregation: How it is affecting America's inner-city schools. Lincoln Memorial University Law Review, 1(2). The Missouri Student Transfer Program 118

Hampe, B. (2007). Making Documentary Films and Videos. New York, NY: A Holt Paperback Henry Holt and Company. Hochschild, J. & Scovronick, N. (2003). The American dream and the public schools. New York: Oxford University Press.

International Journal of Qualitative Methods (2006). Los Angeles: Sage Publishing.

Jacob, B.A. (2007). The challenges of staffing urban schools with effective teachers. The Future of Children, 17(1). 129-153.

Jensen, E. (2009). Teaching with poverty in mind. Alexandria, VA: ASCD. Liddell v. Board of Education, 98 F.R.D. 548 (E.D. Mo. 1983)

Lincoln, Y. & Guba, E. (1985). Naturalistic inquiry. Newbury Park, CA: Sage Publishing.

Medley, K.W. (2003). We as Freemen: Plessy v. Ferguson. Gretna LA: Pelican.

Missouri Census Data Center (2016). Retrieved from: http://mcdc.missouri.edu/
Missouri Department of Elementary and Secondary Education (DESE) (n.d.). Accreditation classification of school districts. Retrieved from: https://dese.mo.gov/quality-schools/moschool-improvementprogram/accreditation-classification-school-districts

Missouri Department of Elementary and Secondary Education (DESE) (2014.). Comprehensive Guide to the Missouri School Improvement Program. Retrieved from: https://dese.mo.gov/sites/default/files/MSIP-5-comprehensive-guide.pdf

Norwood, K.J. (2012). Minnie Liddell's forty-year quest for quality public education remains a dream deferred. Washington University Journal of Law & Policy 40 (1).

Patton, M. Q. (2002). Qualitative research & evaluation methods (3rd ed.). Thousand Oaks, CA: Sage Publishing.

Plessy v. Ferguson (1896). Supreme Court of Louisiana.

Rafsky, S. (2015). Increased risks for filmmakers and sources in documentaries' golden age. Committee to Protect Journalists. Retrieved from: http://cpj.org/x/64fd

Research and Development Corporation (2009). Retrieved from: www.rdc.org

Researcher. 2009. Mirriam-Webster Dictionary.

Roberts v. City of Boston (1850). Massachusetts Supreme Court. Shelley v. Kraemer, 334 U.S. 1 (1948).

Salter, J. &, Hollingsworth, H. (2013). Missouri school transfers to cause financial problems for districts. Retrieved from: The Missouri Student Transfer Program 119 http://www.kansascity.com/news/local/article324480/Missouri-school-transfersto-cause-financial-problems-for-districts.html

Sumner, C. (1849). Argument against the constitutionality of separate colored schools. Boston: B.F. Roberts.

Swann v. Charlotte-Mecklenburg Board of Education, 402 U.S. 1 (1971).

The relationships between school poverty and student achievement in Maine (2014). University of Southern Maine, Portland.

Thomas, J.Y. & Brady, K.P. (2005). The elementary and secondary education act at 40: Equity, accountability, and the evolving federal role in public education. North Carolina State University, Raleigh.

Turner v. School District of Clayton (2010). Circuit Court of St. Louis County.

Uchitelle, S. & Heaney, G.W. (2004). Unending struggle: The long road to an equal education in St. Louis. St. Louis, MO: Reedy Press.

*United States District Court v. Indianapolis Public Schools (1975).

US Commission on Civil Rights (1977). School Segregation in Kirkwood, Missouri.

Voluntary Interdistrict Choice Corporation (2016). Frequently Asked Questions.

ORDER NOW

Available at drhowardfields.com

Made in the USA
Monee, IL
11 May 2024